W9-BMO-673

No Fluff *Guide To*

COPYWRITING

⭐ Spend More Time <u>Writing</u>
Copy That Gets Results
Less Time Learning How To!

By:

DEREK FRANKLIN
www.derekfranklin.com

No Fluff Guide To Copywriting

Spend More Time Writing Copy That Gets Results,
Less Time Learning How To!

By Derek Franklin

www.derekfranklin.com

Table Of Contents

Introduction

If you're looking for a long, drawn-out introduction here – one that goes into detail about the history of copywriting, or why it's an important part of business, then you apparently didn't read the title of this book. This is a *no fluff* guide, and the lack of 'fluffiness' (stuff you really don't need to bother with knowing or learning) begins right here!

That being said, let me take a moment to share with you a couple of things you may actually *want* to know, beginning with...

What's A No Fluff Guide?

In addition to having an overall simple structure, the content of this book is built around a concept known as the Pareto Principle (more commonly referred to as the 80/20 rule), which essentially states that 80% of the best results you achieve in almost any activity in life comes from just 20% of the actions you take.

So, with that in mind, this *No Fluff Guide* is designed to save you valuable time by giving you nothing but the 20% most important and useful ideas and tips that will help you achieve 80% of the best results possible when it comes to holding effective meetings.

If you want *better* results than that, and you're willing to invest the time, this guide has a unique feature (which I'll explain shortly) that will help you with that as well.

Why I Wrote This Simple Guide

It was once said that there is genius in simplicity.

The genius of simple ideas, like the ones you'll discover in this guide, comes from the fact that they are:

- **Easy to learn** - There's very little effort to learn them, so you don't put-off learning them until 'sometime later'

- **Easy to use** - They're practical - you can see yourself actually using them

- **Able to produce dramatic results** - The value of the result *far* outweighs the effort it took to get the result

If you're like me, all 3 of these factors are very appealing, especially in the time-strapped society we live in today.

As a result, I set out on a mission to take the best ideas and information I've discovered about copywriting, and distilled them down into a number of easy-to-consume, digestible bites of useful knowledge that you can begin using immediately in order to achieve some pretty great results!

I had absolutely *no* desire to write an 'encyclopedia' about copywriting – with a fancy layout, fancy graphics, or a lot of other unnecessary nonsense - like a lot of other books you see out there.

Why not?

Because like you, I don't have the time or desire to spend many hours or many days reading a book, any book (including my own), that's likely full of a lot of time-consuming, useless fluff that will do nothing but confuse me or slow me down.

My intention when writing this simple guide was to give readers something they would look at and think, 'that thing is packed full of some really valuable tips and ideas that I *will* be using. I'm glad I have it!'

I sincerely hope that's *your* reaction.

Derek Franklin

How To Get The Most From This No Fluff Guide

This guide is built to help you get results!

The main way it does this is that each item is presented to you in the form of an action statement (you're told to do something). This is meant to subtly engage your mind in a way that encourages you to take progressive, positive action in order to achieve better results.

In addition, in order to maximize the overall value you get from this guide, I'd like to recommend you use the following action plan:

- Read each item carefully. The ideas are concise, so this should be fairly easy to do.

- Highlight and put a number next to any ideas that may be new to you, and you think you would like to implement.

- The next opportunity you get, select just 2-3 of the highlighted items to put in into practice (not too many at once).

- Read/review this guide again every several months to refresh your memory.

Is that a simple, realistic, and practical game-plan, or what?

Using The Related Searches Feature

In most sections of this guide you will see references to *Related Searches*, either in the middle of the section or at the end of it.

These hand-selected searches are meant to point you with a wealth of additional online resources and information about a specific topic.

This allows *you* to decide where you want to expand your knowledge, and where you don't.

In other words, you get the best of both worlds; a quality collection of simple-to-read, easy-to-use ideas and tips about a topic within the guide itself, as well as a number of useful suggestions for how to tap into the largest resource of dynamic and interactive information on the planet – the Web – to dig even deeper into a topic, if you choose to do so.

Let's face it; even if I were to write pages, and pages, and more pages of content about a topic, there's no way that it would even come close to comparing to the wealth of dynamic, interactive content (articles, videos, and tools) you can discover for that topic online using Google and the right search terms.

Here's an example of the *Related Searches* feature, as well as a brief explanation of how to use it:

Related Searches:

tips for saving time – Videos

personal organizer – Shopping

writing | creating a book

business cards [zip code or city name] - Local

- The words to the left of the hash-mark represent the related search terms to try.

- Some search terms contain a *pipe* character (|). This is intentionally included and should be included when you enter the search term into Google (it's above the backslash character [\] on your keyboard). This special character is used to tell Google you want results containing either the term on the left OR the term on the right. In the example above, we're asking Google to show us any results related to *writing a book* OR *creating a book*.

- Some search terms require custom input from you. In the example above, *business cards [zip code or city name]* is indicating that you should enter the terms, *business cards*, followed by your local zip code or city name, such as, *business cards 47401*, or *business cards las vegas*.

- It's recommended that you try each search term using Google's main search page (www.google.com) first. This will provide you with the best overall results.

- The text to the right of the hash-mark indicates other Google search tools to try for those terms. In the examples above, in addition to doing a standard *Google Web* search on the terms shown, you'd want to do a *Google Videos* search for *tips for saving time*, and a *Google Shopping* search for *personal organizer*. You can find links to these other tools at the top of most Google search pages.

- When you see the *Related Searches* feature used in the middle of a section, this means that the searches are related to the specific tip just above it. Related Searches shown at the end of a section indicate searches that are related to the overall topic, or section.

Why Copywriting Is So Great!

- **It's Total Freedom** - Freedom is often associated with most jobs that allow you to work from home, and copywriting is no different. In order to be a copywriter these days, you need little more than a computer and an Internet connection, which means you can essentially work from anywhere in the world, any time you want. Now *that's* freedom!

- **You're Already Halfway To Becoming An Expert** - Copywriting is nothing more than taking a skill that you already know, and you've been developing since you were 2 - writing - and fine-tuning it a little. Because you already understand the mechanics of writing (how words fit together, what they mean, how to punch keys on a keyboard), the only thing you really need to learn is how to put that skill to use in a very purposeful, emotional, attention-grabbing way, which is actually a lot of fun.

- **You're Always Learning New Things** - Each copywriting project requires you to 'get into the skin' of your reader. This usually requires learning new things, thinking new ways, and exploring new possibilities - things that are outside of your normal, routine life. Like an actor, who takes on roles that allow him to temporarily experience the adventure of becoming a different person, copywriting allows you to do something very similar, but express it a different way (writing about it instead of physically acting it out).

- **You Experience The Satisfaction Of Positive Results** - One of the best reasons for expressing creativity has always been to see the impact that your thoughts, ideas, and creations can have on the lives of others. When you write great copy, the results you see show up in the form of satisfied, excited clients, as well as readers, who's lives you're changing in positive ways.

- **You've Got What Everybody Wants** - Copywriting is everywhere these days, from the front of book covers, to the words used in commercials. Companies of all sizes understand the incredible power well-crafted words have in getting attention and moving people to take action. That's what drives business, and that's what drives them to your front door.

- **Something Magical Happens To Your Brain** - When you consistently write emotional, attention-grabbing copy, the result is more than just words on a page. This form of writing alters your mindset in some pretty powerful ways, too. You learn, almost at a subconscious level, how to emotionally connect with others better, how to understand their challenges, and how to share with them solutions that can have a considerable impact on their lives. These skills will serve you well in all areas of your life and business.

- **Opportunity Keeps On Knockin'** - Once you feel comfortable with the process of writing in a way that impacts people, you can easily expand your opportunities by creating and selling products of your own (no one says you have to write for someone else the rest of your life). This puts you in total control of your time, the projects you work on, and how much money you want to make.

- **More Results = More Money** - Businesses want results; better sales, more people joining their mailing list, or more people requesting information about their products and services. If you can deliver these kinds of results, consistently, they'll gladly you pay you quite nicely. It's a total win/win!

Before You Write

Collect Information

Do Your Research

- **Appreciate The Importance Of Good Research** - Research gives you focus and clarity about the project you're working on - it helps you fill the gaps of your knowledge, which is essential for doing a quality, efficient job.

- **Research Your Product** – Discover:

  - What's it made of?

  - Why was it created?

  - When was it discovered?

  - Who discovered it?

  - What's it based on?

  - How is it made?

- **Get It Straight From The Horses Mouth** - Talk to the person who created the product - the founder, developer, or whoever it may be. Ask them lots of well thought-out questions, and listen closely to their answers, and take plenty of notes.

- **Try It First-Hand** - Ask for samples of the product, so you and others can try it out. This will help you internalize the need for the product, as well as its benefits.

- **Research The Company** - Find out as much as you can about the company that creates the product you're promoting. What's their mission statement, achievements, and history?

- **Ask For Existing Marketing Materials** - Study past promotions, both those that worked, and those that didn't. Try to figure out the emotions, words, and images that made one promo work and the other not.

- **Ask For Testimonials** - Study testimonials and try to figure out the core benefits and emotions that the majority of users are expressing their feelings about. This will provide valuable insight into the approach you should take with your writing. Some may even provide inspiration for your main headline.

- **Study The Competition's Marketing Materials** - Successful competitors usually have successful promotions. Look them over to determine what elements stand out and seem to work well.

- **Go Online** - Fire up your browser and gather facts, statistics, and interesting stories about the product, the company that makes it, or the industry that the product targets. For example, if the product targets people interested in green living, search *Google* for *green living facts*, *green living statistics*, or *green living forums* to see what sorts of things people are discussing that might prove helpful in your writing.

- **Get The Price** - Of course, it's necessary to know the price of the product before you begin writing your copy, but dig deeper and find out the reasons behind the price being what it is. What are others charging for something similar, and what went into creating the product that justifies the price?

- **Discover Objections** - Ask for a list of objections about the product that have been expressed in the past. It's crucial that your copy addresses each of the one's that are commonly used.

Determine Your Copy's Purpose

- **Determine Your Copy's Purpose** - Is it to:

    - Get the reader to purchase today?

    - Get the reader to enter their email address?

    - Get the reader to request more information?

- **Focus On Your Purpose** - Once you've determined the purpose of your copy, be sure to focus your overall approach (the things you write, your testimonials, graphics, etc.) on accomplishing that one thing.

Get Your Client Involved

- **Agree On A USP** - A product's unique value to the reader (USP) is essential for providing guidance on how the copy should be written. Don't wait until you've spent a lot of time writing your copy before getting input about the USP from the client. They may point you in a totally different direction than what you expected, causing a lot of wasted time and money.

- **Agree On A Sales Message** - Before writing, share with the client the approach you intend to take with your copy. Get their feedback, or at the very least, check to see if it excites them and they're on board with it.

- **Put Together A Bio** - Get information about your client's experience, accreditation, awards, and all other accolades. Not only will this be helpful as you craft your copy, but it prevent you from bothering them with related questions down the road.

- **Discover Their WHY** - Have your client describe the benefits of their product in as much detail as they possibly can. Ask them who they think their market is, and why.

Develop Your USP

- **Identify What Makes Your Product Different** - How is the product:

  - Unique

  - Easier to use

  - Simpler

  - More efficient

  - Cheaper

  - Smaller

  - Faster

  - More visually appealing

  - A better value

  - A better design

  - More durable

  - More available

  - More widely accepted

  - More comprehensive

  - More time-tested

  - Of higher quality

  - Cutting-edge

- Patented

- **Follow These Guidelines** - An effective USP is:

  - **Short** - The fewer the words, the better.

  - **Positive** - Saying, "We've never made a customer mad" might convey good customer service, but in a negative way. Find a positive way to state the same thing.

  - **Centered Around An Emotional Benefit** - "You get younger-looking skin" is better than "It moisturizes your skin."

  - **Memorable** - "Just do it"

  - **Original** - Things such as a low price, great service, and 50 years in business are all overdone, boring, and ineffective. You sometimes have to put a new twist on old ideas.

- **Prove It** - Use statistics, testimonials, and charts to provide proof that you can deliver on your USP.

- **Deliver It** - Only make a promise in your USP if you can deliver it!

- **Make Good Use Of Your USP** - Reinforce the main idea behind your USP throughout your copy.

Related Searches:

creating a usp – Videos

usp tips - <u>Videos</u>

Get To Know Your Reader

- **Bridge The Gap** - You must bridge the gap between what the reader already knows, and what's new to them (what you're offering them). To bridge the gap, you have to know what your reader already knows.

- **Become The Reader** - Sit quietly and imagine yourself as the reader - get into their skin and answer these questions:

    - What is their mindset? The who's, what's, where's, when's, and why's?

    - What are their fears and joys?

    - What are their wants and issues?

    - Where do they live?

    - What products, especially related products, have they purchased in the past?

    - What year were they born, when did they go through high school? What cultural references are they familiar with (including events, fads, people, music, etc.)?

    - What are their beliefs, values, and traditions?

    - What is their income? Is it fixed, seasonal, going up, going down?

    - What is their mental and emotional state?

- What kinds of 'movies' play in their head about their life, abilities, reputation, and self-worth?

- What is their predisposition (willing to listen or very skeptical), expectations, mood (happy, tired, or frustrated), and environment (home or work) the moment they encounter your marketing message.

- Are they sick of the same old marketing tactics?

- What's the conversation going on in their head about the problem your product will solve?

Related Searches:

personality traits list

personality traits of women

personality traits of men

Prepare To Write: Establish A Routine

- **Write On Schedule** - Set aside a specific time each day to write.

- **Write In 30 Minute Blocks** - Use a timer and block out at least 30 minute sections where you'll do nothing but write. Don't let anything break your flow, including bathroom breaks, getting a drink, eating...*NOTHING*! Try to fit at least 6 of these into your day.

- **Write At Your Peak** - Make sure you write during *your* peak creativity period, whether that's in the morning, afternoon, or night.

- **Write Every Day** - You've got to be consistent with your writing. You'll accomplish more by writing 10 minutes a day than you will writing 8 hours once every couple weeks.

- **Prepare For Tomorrow, Today** - Before ending your day, make a list of things you want to accomplish tomorrow. Then, gather everything together that you need make it happen. Putting things in place ahead of time will increase your chances of getting them done!

- **Use Personal Deadlines** - Set personal deadlines that are within the deadlines set by clients. Get projects done before they *have* to be done.

Related Searches:

writing routine

Prepare To Write: Get Into The Flow

- **Eliminate Distractions** - Turn off all electronic distractions while you write - phone, email, instant messaging applications, and browser windows.

  Related Searches:

  eliminate distractions

- **Write, Write, Write** - Get into a flow of writing without stopping or judging what you're writing, or worrying about grammar, formatting, or adding slick copywriting techniques. Writing in a flow like this will provide a priceless number of ideas to select and build upon.

- **Talk & Record** - Start talking about your product or service and record your ideas and thoughts into a voice recorder. Use these for inspiration when creating your copy.

  Related Searches:

  voice recorder - Shopping

  voice recorder reviews

- **Use Flow To Achieve One Voice** - Try to write as much as you can in a single sitting. This allows you to easily maintain the same voice and attitude throughout your copy.

Prepare To Write: Organize Your Work Area

- **Keep It Clean & Uncluttered** - Keep your work area, especially your desk, clear of stacks of papers and magazines, used dishes, knick-knacks, batteries, or anything else that doesn't need to be there for you to write and take care of your daily tasks. Don't allow your desk to become a catch-all location for 'stuff.' Whether you know it or not, physical clutter that you see is a constant reminder of tasks that are left undone, and it becomes a constant mental distraction.

Related Searches:

unclutter your desk

- **Maintain An Orderly Desk** - Establish a single location to store pens and pencils, post-it notes, or any other items you use regularly, and always keep them there.

Related Searches:

organize your desk

- **Get A Nice Chair** - Writing for hours usually requires sitting for hours. You should get the most comfortable chair you can afford. For something new, go to *Google* and do a search for *computer chairs*. For something used and inexpensive, go to *www.craigslist.org* to search for *computer chairs* for sale in your area.

- **Keep A Notepad Handy** - You never know when a great idea will hit you. Always keep a notepad within reach so you can quickly capture ideas that come to you. Then, immediately get back to what you were doing.

- **Eliminate Background Distractions** - Don't fool yourself into thinking that a TV on in the background, or your neighbors barking dog, will not affect your writing...they will! Turn off the TV, get earplugs, and do whatever else you can do to quiet the world around you so you can focus on writing great copy!

Related Searches:

earplugs - Shopping

stop your neighbor's dog from barking

Prepare To Write: Maintain Your Computer

- **Defragment Regularly** - Defragmenting your computer's hard drive is similar to organizing files in a file cabinet, so you can find and use them more efficiently. If you don't take care of this step (especially on a computer running Microsoft Windows), your computer can begin to slow down over time. Windows has a built-in disk defragmenter, which does a sufficient job, but for best results, use a 3rd-party tool (look for suggestions below).

  Related Searches:

  how to defragment your computer - <u>Videos</u>

  disk defragmenter download

  disk defragmenter reviews - <u>Videos</u>

- **Maintain Virus Protection** - A single virus can bring down your computer, and can bring it down for good. If your computer is at the core of your business, this could result in some pretty substantial losses. DO NOT neglect using antivirus software! If you're using Microsoft Windows, I recommend their excellent antivirus tool, which you can find by doing a *Google* search for *microsoft security essentials*.

  Related Searches:

  microsoft security essentials - <u>Videos</u>

  antivirus software - <u>Shopping</u>

free antivirus software

antivirus software reviews - Videos

- **Backup Regularly** - Hard drives crash, and with a nasty crash, there go all your files! It's crucial that you're always prepared for this possibility by regularly backing up your hard drive. This usually requires having a second (sometimes external) drive, and a piece of software that automatically, and regularly copies files from your main hard drive to your second one.

Related Searches:

how to back up computer - Videos

backup software - Videos

online backup - Videos

backup software review - Videos

external hard drive - Shopping

external hard drive review

- **Get Rid Of Unused Stuff** - Over time, you add things to your computer that you end up no longer needing or using. These unwanted items clutter up your hard drive, your computer's desktop, and sometimes use up your computer's resources (especially memory) without you knowing it. At least once a month, remove unused shortcuts from your desktop, and uninstall software you no longer use.

Related Searches:

how to uninstall software - Videos

- **Clean The Mouse & Keyboard** - Germs and filth that build up on your keyboard and mouse could make you sick, which brings a halt to your productivity. Schedule a regular time each month to clean these parts of your computer, to give yourself a better chance of staying healthy.

Related Searches:

how to clean your keyboard - <u>Videos</u>

how to clean your mouse - <u>Videos</u>

how to clean your monitor - <u>Videos</u>

clean your laptop - <u>Videos</u>

Related Searches:

maintain your computer - <u>Videos</u>

speed up your computer - <u>Videos</u>

Prepare To Write: Maintain Your Health

- **Plan For Sleep** - Writing good copy requires a clear head. Get plenty of rest before writing copy, and save staying up late for some other time.

  Related Searches:

  sleeping tips - <u>Videos</u>

  how to sleep better - <u>Videos</u>

- **Eat The Right Food** - Avoid sugar or fat-laden foods and drinks before writing copy. It's better to stick with fruits, teas, and good ol' water.

  Related Searches:

  how to eat for energy

- **Start Your Day Early** - Starting your day early in the morning allows you to work when things are usually the quietest, and if you take advantage of it, you can feel the incredible satisfaction that comes by accomplishing more by noon than most people do all day!

- **Really Enjoy Yourself Regularly** - Take plenty of time AWAY from work to have fun and enjoy quality time with your friends and family. Contrary to popular belief, regular periods of rest and recreation contribute more to being productive than if you simply work all the time.

- **Get Moving** - Start a simple exercise program. Even walking on a treadmill for 5 minutes a day can result in a decent increase of energy and clarity that will help you in the writing process (always consult your physician).

Related Searches:

simple | easy | creative ways to exercise

desk exercises - <u>Videos</u>

- **Practice Deep Breathing** - Get into the habit of taking several slow, deep breaths of fresh air before you begin writing. Oxygen will help you think more clearly.

Related Searches:

deep breathing exercises - <u>Videos</u>

- **Put Yourself In A Positive State** - Put yourself in a peak positive state by focusing on something positive that you absolutely love or look forward to doing - get excited about it! Jump up and down if you want! Or stand up, take several deep breaths and say 'YES!' several times with enthusiasm and power. Watching something funny can also be a great way to put you in a positive state for maximum creativity.

- **Take A Break Occasionally** - Take at least a 5 minute break for every 30 minutes of work. Spend that 5 minutes thinking about anything (your upcoming vacation, how much fun you had over the weekend, etc.) other than your work.

Prepare To Write:
Create An Outline

- **Start With An Outline** - Use an outline tool or mind map to create a 'skeleton' of the overall direction you want to take with your copy, then go back and add some muscle to it! Your outline should contain sections for these basic elements:

  - Headline

  - Subheadlines

  - Bullets

  - Testimonials

  - Guarantee

  - Call to action

  - Disclaimers

Related Searches:

outliner software - Shopping

mind mapping software - Shopping

what is mind mapping - Images, Videos

- **Build Out Your Outline** - Attach relevant ideas and research to appropriate areas of your outline as you come across them.

- **Tackle One Section At A Time** - Once your outline is complete, set aside a specific block of time to work on each section of it. This will provide you with a useful schedule to reference to make sure you're on-track to hit your overall project deadline.

The Copywriter's Mindset

Tap Into Emotions

- **Sell To Emotion** - People buy on emotion and then use logic to justify their decision. Emotional impact is better than statistical impact. Both are important, but facts and figures are secondary to reaching someone on an emotional level.

- **Appeal To Desires** - Understand what emotional element you're selling:

  - You don't sell a car - you sell recognition

  - You don't sell insurance - you sell security

  - You don't sell vitamins - you sell perfect health and energy

- **Paint A Vivid Picture** - Include words in your copy that involve all 5 senses. People pay attention to anything that stimulates their senses. Include lots of details to make the end-result of using your product crystal clear. Put your reader into the center of the scene.

- **Create A Virtual Experience** - It's been proven that if a consumer 'touches' a product, they instantly get a stronger sense of ownership. Help your reader 'virtually' touch and experience your product with the words you write.

- **Agitate Then Solve** - Help the reader vividly imagine the pain of the problem your product solves, then help them feel the pleasure of the solution.

- **Convey Action** - Use action words (running, looking, searching, relaxing, etc.) to help stimulate emotion in your reader.

- **Tap Into The Desire To Belong** - People have a desire to belong to a specific group - people they feel are their peers. This is often what motivates their decisions about what clothes they wear, music they listen to, activities they take part in, and so on. Give your reader a chance to be a part of a group that they want to be part of.

- **Make Your Offer Sound Exclusive** - Use the terms 'membership' or 'members-only privileges' in relation to your offer. This is an invitation for them to join, while seemingly excluding others.

- **Use Celebrity** - When possible, show how respected, high-profile individuals in the readers desired peer group are using your product.

- **Appeal To Your Reader's Fears** - Appealing to fears gets results because it paints a picture of a necessary response. Appeal to these fears:

  - **Failure** - Not living up to their full potential; Not experiencing and enjoying the life they could have had.

  - **Rejection** - Looking like a fool or idiot in the eyes of others for not doing something the 'right way.'

  - **Physical harm & death** - Having to experience something that causes physical pain, or death, either immediately or gradually.

  - **Missing an opportunity** - Looking back with hindsight and realizing how they may have passed up the opportunity of a lifetime.

- **Loss** - Loosing something they currently have and cherish (money, independence, friends, happiness).

- **Things that affect loved ones** - Fears related to things that affect loved ones, which is more powerful than fears the reader personally has. For example, saying, "These foods may be destroying your kids' health" is more emotionally powerful than, "These foods may be destroying YOUR health."

- **Use Curiosity** - Humans have a built-in desire to get complete answers. When the brain has a vacancy, it needs to be filled! Use curiosity to suck your reader into your copy, and get them to continue reading:

  - **Tell them you have a secret** - Everyone loves to have something special revealed to them.

  - **Make a statement that's incomplete** - "I was about to give up my dream of dancing, and then I discovered something that changed the course of my life..."

  - **Use questions, but don't answer them right away** - Our brains love discovering answers to questions, especially if finding the answer only involves reading the rest of the page.

- **Provide valuable information, but only half of it** - Tell the reader something valuable, then tell them the action they must take to get the rest of the info (continue reading, enter their email, download a special report, etc.)

- **Use absolutes to create a burning curiosity** - Use words such as 'never' or 'always', as in, "You should NEVER do this with your money - EVER!"

- **Use juxtaposition** - Add things together that seemingly don't belong together. "I had to lose everything before I discovered how rich I was!"

- **Use Vanity** - Use vanity when your product or service appeals to a characteristic that society considers desirable, such as personal power or physical attractiveness.

Related Searches:

emotional copywriting

Focus On One Idea

- **Remember That Focus Creates Clarity** - Focusing on a single idea in your copy eliminates potential confusion and allows you to connect with your reader at a deeper, and more persuasive level.

- **Ring The Bell** - Occasionally, subtly remind your reader of the idea.

Use AIDA: Attention, Interest, Desire, & Action

Attention

- Attract attention to your headline and opening paragraph

- Tap into your reader's emotions

- Don't discuss your product, discuss a sought-after benefit

- Make your headline visually stand out

Interest

- Use plenty of benefits tied with a lot of emotion

- Include subheadlines and lots of scannable bullet points

- Let the reader know how you can fulfill their dreams

- Talk about the negative results from not taking action

Desire

- Touch on the desirable end-benefits that come from getting your product

- Paint a vivid picture of the end-result of you're offer - include plenty of details and appeal to all the senses

- Show how your product is the total solution to each one of the reader's needs

Action

- Get the reader to take action now!

- Use scarcity - a limited time, a limited number, or a limited offer

- Provide valuable bonuses for taking action now

- ASK the reader to click the order button (or fill out the order form)

- Provide specific instructions about the ordering process - what they will get, when they can expect it, etc.

Related Searches:

aida formula

Use Front-Loading

- **Understand Why It's Important** – People scan information, starting at the top, or the beginning – tops of pages, tops of bulleted lists, the beginning of sentences, etc. You must put the most important information in these locations.

- **Front-Load Your Copy Elements** - Front-load everything with the most important information at the top, or at the beginning:

  > - **The sales page itself** - The top of the page always contains the most important front-loaded element - your headline
  >
  > - **Paragraphs** - Put the most important idea of the paragraph in the first sentence.
  >
  > - **Sentences** - Put the most important words of the sentence at its beginning
  >
  > - **Bulleted lists** - Put the most important bullet point at the top of each bulleted list
  >
  > - **Words in a bullet point** - Grab the reader with the first few words in each bullet point

Answer 'What's In It For Me?'

- **Answer The 'Why'** - Your readers are all asking the same question, 'why?', and you need to always provide them with a REASON why. Studies have shown that people are more likely to go along with a request if you simply give them a reason why they should, even if the reason you give them makes no sense. Be sure to answer the 'why':

    - Why are you targeting me with this product or service? Of what benefit is it to me?

    - Why should I listen to, and believe you? What are your credentials?

    - Why was your product or service created? What challenge does it address, and why should I care?

    - Why should I continue reading this? Is this just to sell me something, or am I going to discover something of value?

    - What's the sense in buying this now? Why are there limited copies, a limited time to order, or a limited offer?

    - Why is your price what it is? What makes you think it's worth that?

- **Lose The 'I'** - Change 'I' statements to 'you' statements.

Be Honest And Truthful

- **Live By A Standard Of Truth** - Honesty is ALWAYS the best policy!

- **Value Truth** - Honesty and truth lead to trust, which is one of the most essential ingredients for turning a reader into a customer.

- **Remember, A Lie Is A Lie** - False statements or lies are magnified in peoples' minds more than truths. Even a little dishonesty can have huge, negative consequences.

- **Don't Try To Convince People Of Your Honesty** - Never say, "let me be honest with you" (or similar). Whenever you blatantly attempt to convince your audience of a conclusion ('I'm honest', 'I'm funny', or 'trust me') they tend to believe the opposite. It's as if you're saying, let me *tell* this conclusion, because typically, my actions prove otherwise.

- **Keep It Believable** - Make sure your copy sounds believable. This means you should avoid hype and exaggerations of any kind.

- **If It Sounds Unbelievable, Give Plenty Of Proof** - Back up *seemingly* outrageous statements with plenty of credible proof.

- **Be Congruent** - Make sure the things you say in your copy are congruent, from start to finish. Inconsistencies, even subtle ones, kill trust and credibility.

- **Make Good On Your Promises** - If you make a promise to reveal something in your headline or other parts of your copy, be sure to reveal it.

- **Honor Your Guarantee** - This should go without saying, but you should always honor your guarantee, promptly and pleasantly. Stand behind your promises.

- **Don't Lie With Photos** - Don't use stock photos of people within your testimonials, and don't alter a photo in any way that is deceptive (for example, cropping isn't usually a deceptive edit) unless you disclose that you have.

Watch Your Words

- **Strive For Short & Simple** - Use shorter, simple words that can express the same meaning as complex words and phrases; use one-syllable words when possible.

- **Take Out The Fluff** - Get rid of unnecessary words like adjectives, adverbs, "in," etc.

- **Take It Easy!** - Use exclamation points (!) where appropriate, but as little as possible.

- **Use Emotionally-Appealing Words** - Choose words with a similar meaning but more emotional impact:

  - Not *cost*, but *investment*

  - Not *products*, but *solutions*

  - Not *house*, but *home*

  - Not *deal*, but *opportunity*

  - Not *learn*, but *discover*

  - Not *buy now*, but *add to cart*

- **Use Positive Phrases** - Use positive words in place of their negative counterparts when describing your product or service:

  - Not *inexpensive* or *cheap*, but *economical*

  - Not *free of pesticides*, but *100% organic and safe*

- **Lose The Stuffiness** - Use common, informal words in place of their more 'fancy' counterparts:

> • Not *dwelling*, but *home*
>
> • Not *digital device*, but *gadget*

- **Replace The Buts** - Use *and* instead of *but* - use *and* to focus on a positive:

> • Not, "This exercise program works, but you have to make time to follow-through" but, "This exercise program works, and it only takes 20 minutes a day, three times a week "

- **Use Gender-Neutral Terms** - Because you'll likely be writing to both men and women, use gender-neutral terms in order to appeal to both groups:

> • Not *spokesman*, but *spokesperson*

- **Check For Pet Words** - Minimize your use of 'pet words', or words you tend to overuse. Most modern word processors allow you to run a report that will display the most commonly used words in a document. Run a report and edit your copy where necessary.

- **Forget The Jargon** -Be aware of using jargon that your reader may not understand. If it's not understood, jargon can create a point of confusion in the reader's mind, which could lead them to tuning out your message for good!

- **Convey Confidence** - Avoid using tentative adjectives, which suck the conviction out of your copy - things such as, 'pretty good', 'fairly decent', or 'quite tasty'. Just say, 'good', 'decent', or 'tasty'.

- **Inject Some Action** - Give your copy a sense of movement - use lots of action words.

- **Avoid Cliches** - Using cliches makes your copy seem old, predictable, and unexciting.

Related Searches:

most persuasive words

words that sell list

Use The Most Powerful, Persuasive Words

Include the following words in your copy to make it more persuasive:

- **Discover** - When you tell people they're going to discover something (as opposed to 'learning' it), it triggers a sense of adventure and excitement, as if they're about to start on a journey to find a hidden treasure.

- **Easy** - People feel their lives are too hard and complicated as it is. When you offer them something that will not only improve their lives, but it's easy to do, it becomes very desirable.

- **Guarantee** - Most people don't like being risk-takers. A guarantee goes a long way to eliminating any fears or doubts they may have about taking action on your offer.

- **Health** - If people don't have their health, very few other things matter. Your reader's health is of prime importance to them, so anything that can help improve it is something that gets their attention.

- **Money** - In the minds of most people, money represents freedom - freedom to do what they want, when they want to do it. This kind of lifestyle is often a high priority.

- **New** - When something is new, it's considered fresh, up-to-date, based on new research and technology, and is certainly better than the old thing.

- **Proven** - When something has been proven, it's shown itself to be reliable, and of high quality.

- **Results** - Results are the bottom-line that your reader wants. It's the main reason they read your copy and buy your product.

- **Safe** - This word brings a sense of comfort and peace of mind.

- **Save** - It's usually easier for your reader to keep what they already have than it is to make more, so the idea of saving time, money, or anything else, is understood as a way to get results with very little effort.

- **You** - Using this word helps keep the focus on the main beneficiary of the results promised - the reader.

- **Love** - Love is the strongest emotion any of us feel. We crave it, and will do almost anything to experience. It has power!

- **Free** - When something is given as free, it feels like a gift that someone wants to give them - outside the suspicion that comes from asking for something in return.

- **Own** - Owning something implies they have it now, and are using and benefiting from it. This is much better than buying, which implies they're giving up something (their money) to get it.

- **Best** - There's nothing higher or better than something that is the best. It conveys the idea that they need nothing else but this.

Tell Stories

- **Appreciate The Value Of Telling Stories** – Readers love stories that are inspirational, informative and easy to share with others. Stories are generally easy to remember, connect with the reader on an emotional level, and help the reader appreciate what's possible.

- **Keep Them Short** - The longer the story, the greater the chance your reader won't stick around to finish it. When relating a story, keep it simple, short, and concise.

- **Focus On A Single Idea** - When telling a story, determine the main point or lesson you want to convey, then edit your storytelling in a way that weaves that point or lesson through the story as you tell it.

- **Include Plenty Of Details** - Details bring a story to life and make it more believable. Include details about numbers, dates, days of the week, names, etc.

- **Appeal To All The Senses** - A memorable and emotionally-appealing story is one that taps into as many of the senses as possible. As you tell a story, describe the sensory experience in detail.

- **Share A Personal Story** - The best stories you can tell are usually the ones that have a deep, personal meaning to you. Because it happened to you, sharing the details and emotions that make it a great story comes almost naturally. People will also appreciate how you're speaking from first-hand experience, which makes what you say more believable.

Related Searches:

storytelling tips - <u>Videos</u>

how to tell a story

Connect With The Reader

- **Build Trust** - The more the reader connects with you, the more they'll trust you. Trust is KEY! You want to convey: "I'm just like you!"

Become The Reader's Advocate

- **Discover Their Source Of Pain** - Find out what enemy is making your reader feel powerless, insulted, frustrated and angry. Is it the banks, doctors, drug companies, the tax man?

- **Discover Their Reason For Pain** - Learn what causes the enemy to make your reader angry. Is it because they lie, cheat, or treat them like an ignorant idiot? Are they arrogant, or selfish?

- **Recognize & Validate Their Feelings** - Acknowledge your reader's frustrations. Validate their sense of powerlessness about the challenge you're offering to solve.

- **Get Passionate** - Say everything your reader would love to tell the enemy. Get angry, get emotional, get edgy, use emotionally-charged words.

- **Let Them Know You're Just Like Them** - Tell them that you've been in their shoes (if you have) and that you understand where they're coming from: "I know how you feel."

- **Get The Reader Positively Excited** - Write so that the reader is nodding their head, maybe even laughing, as they read, realizing how true your words are.

- **Give Them Relief** - Reveal to the reader how your solution will permanently relieve their negative feelings.

Be Conversational

- **Write In A Voice Your Reader Connects With** - Use words and phrases they use, in a language they understand. If you're selling to farmers, sound like a farmer.

- **Remember That Grammar Is Secondary** - Perfect grammar is *not* important - a good rhythm and flow to your copy is. Don't be afraid to do things that are generally considered grammar no-no's, if it makes your copy more conversational.

- **Use Contractions** - It's better to use 'don't' than it is to use 'do not'. Using contractions make your copy sound more conversational.

- **Make It Intimate** - Write as if you're writing to one person - a friend, not many.

- **Focus On The Reader** - Avoid using 'I' and 'we' as much as possible. Use 'you' instead, and use it a lot.

- **Keep It Simple** - Use simple words, simple sentences, and simple paragraphs.

- **Avoid Superiority** - Never talk down to your reader or sound condescending.

Include Plenty Of Details & Specificity

- **Use Details To Build Trust** - Details and specifics are more convincing than generalities because they provide a ring of truth and validity to your copy, which are essential for building trust. Generalities arouse suspicion. When quoting facts and figures, be exact.

- **Use Details To Imply Quality** - Details and specifics show the reader your attention to detail (you're not sloppy), implying that what you're offering must also be of high quality.

- **Assume Nothing** - Don't assume your reader knows anything about what you're telling them. Explain in clear detail anything that is new or unusual.

- **Detail Everything** - Include details with:

  - **Numbers** – Not "6000 copies sold" but, "6127 copies sold"

  - **Dates** - Not "in 1937" but, "on June 12, 1937"

  - **Peoples' names** - Not "a guy named Bob" but, "an older guy named Robert J. Smith"

  - **Names of places** - Not "a town in Indiana" but, "a small town in Indiana known as Story"

  - **Facts & Figures** - Not "a study from the 90's showed that over 10,000 people" but, "a 1993 study showed that 10,259 people"

- **Times** - Not "I showed up at 10" but, "I showed up at 10:13 PM"

Emphasize Benefits, Not Features

- **Understand The Difference** - Features and benefits are different in the following ways:

  - Features are what a thing is, technically; Benefits are what it will do for someone, emotionally

  - Benefits answer the question, 'why is this important to me, and why do I need to take action?'

  - Features tell me about 'your x'; Benefits tell me about 'my x'

  - People don't buy products (features), they buy results (benefits)!

  - Feature: Unlimited undo; Benefit: No more worrying about making mistakes

  - Feature: Batteries included; Benefit: Begin using it right away

  - Feature: Detailed statistics; Benefit: Make smarter decisions

  - Feature: 40 miles per gallon; Benefit: Save money

  - Feature: 100% recycled; Benefit: You're helping protect the environment

- **Understand What Benefits Do** - Benefits can be anything that:

> - Saves something (time, energy, resources)
>
> - Improves something (knowledge, self-image, experience)
>
> - Creates/makes something (money, holes in wood, attention)

- **Pile On The Benefits** - Create a list of as many benefits as possible to include in your copy - even the smallest things. The longer the list, the more perceived value your product will have in the eyes of your reader.

- **Generate Benefits From Experience** - The best way to create a list of compelling benefits is to know your product inside and out! Use it and experience it for yourself.

- **Focus On The Future** - Focus on discussing *future* benefits, not benefits they've lost by not using your product or service up to this point (although you can mention them).

Related Searches:

features vs benefits - Videos

benefits vs features marketing - Videos

Watch Your Sentence Structure

- **Write Sentences That *Want* To Be Read** - Make sure your sentences are:

  - Short

  - Simple

  - Focus on a single idea

  - Answers, 'why should I care?'

- **Assume They're Sold** - Write as if your reader is already an active user of your product or service:

  - Not "You could get the whitest teeth you've had in 20 years." but, "Your teeth are whiter and brighter than they have been in 20 years."

  - Not "If you begin using our product..." but, "When you begin using our product..."

- **Write Using An Active Voice** - Create sentences where the subject of the sentence is performing an action, not receiving an action. This style of writing creates a greater sense of action and motion, is easier to read, and usually requires fewer words to explain the same idea:

- Not "The car [subject] is being driven [receiving an action] by Bob" but, "Bob [subject] is driving [performing an action] the car"

- Not "The pencil [subject] was sharpened [receiving an action] by the student" but, "The student [subject] sharpened [performing an action] the pencil"

Related Searches:

active voice and passive voice - <u>Videos</u>

writing in an active voice

- **Use The Bucket Brigade** - Include a word or phrase at the end of one paragraph that motivates the reader to WANT to read the next paragraph; end your paragraphs with a cliffhanger:

  - "More about that later..."

  - "Here's the deal..."

  - "So let me ask you..."

  - "What's the catch?"

  - "Just think that about that for a minute..."

  - "Now picture this..."

  - "Then it hit me..."

  - "And that's just the beginning..."

- **Give Your Sentences Flow & Rhythm** - When you end a sentence with an idea, make sure the sentence that follows it picks up on the previous idea immediately:

> "Do you like red sports cars?
>
> These kinds of cars get noticed and are a ton of fun to drive.
>
> There are very few things that are more fun than to go from 0-60 in 4 seconds flat!
>
> That kind of quickness easily gets addictive.
>
> That's an addiction you can probably live with, right?"

- **Use The Power Of 3** - The *Power Of 3* refers to the technique of using three words, three phrases, or three sentences in a row, in order to emphasize an idea and make it memorable. It works because our minds are tuned to the rhythm of things that come in 3's:

  - "It's as easy as 1-2-3"

  - John Fitzgerald Kennedy (3 names)

  - "Your dog will look better (1), feel better (2), and experience overall better health (3)."

- **Use It Sparingly** - Don't overuse *The Power Of 3* in your copy or it will become obvious, and less effective.

Give Away Value

- **Give Away Results First** - When you can prove something to be true to your reader *before* they buy (in the form of a video tutorial, report, or series of strategies), they immediately gain confidence and trust in anything else you tell them.

- **Create A Sense Of Reciprocation** - When you give something of value away to others for free, it creates a bond of reciprocation, where the receiver becomes more compelled to offer something of value back - usually in the form of cash through the purchase of one of your products or services.

- **Let Them Know You Want To Give Them Something Valuable** - Use a headline that gets your reader to want to 'learn' from your page rather than prompting them to buy something.

- **Make It Something Awesome** - Share with your reader one of your best secrets or techniques - something they can use immediately to see results.

Make A Damaging Confession

- **Appreciate The Power Of A Damaging Confession -** Admitting a flaw of some sort conveys a sense of honesty about you in your reader's mind because dishonest people don't usually admit to doing dumb or bad things. When you make a damaging confession, you're telling your reader that you're no better than they are.

- **Share Your History** - Tell them how you used to be, live, or work. Explain, in detail, the struggles you had, how you couldn't seem to get things right, and how you failed along the way.

- **Be Honest** - Always use a legitimate, honest goof. Don't make one up!

- **Turn Your Confession Into Something Positive** - Turn your damaging confession into a benefit. Explain what lesson you learned, or why it was a good thing that it happened.

Use Repetition, Repetition, Repetition

- **Get Results Through Repetition** - Repetition plays a key role in training your brain to remember and believe something. Use this powerful tool in your copy.

- **Focus On A Single Idea** - Determine the main idea you want to get across, and make that idea the focus of your repetition.

- **Use This Simple Repetition Formula** - Tell them what you're going to tell them, tell them, and then tell them what you told them.

- **Try Different Perspectives** - Find captivating ways to make your point in various ways; by using a direct statement, by providing an example, through telling a story, visually, through a testimonial, and so on.

- **Keep It In Check** - Don't be overly repetitive to the point of being annoying.

Use Metaphors

- **Understand Why Metaphors Work** - Metaphors help paint pictures in your reader's mind. A great metaphor allows you to tie what you're telling them with something they already know, understand, and believe:

  - "Life is a roller coaster"

  - "He was drowning in money"

- **Avoid Cliches** - A metaphor loses a lot of its effectiveness when it's nothing more than a cliche. When tempted to use a metaphor like this, think about how you can put a new, original twist on an old favorite:

  - "He was drowning in money" becomes, "He was consumed by an avalanche of cash"

- **Use Metaphors To Clarify** - There are few times when a good metaphor comes in more handy then when you need to explain something abstract, unfamiliar, or complex. As you write, think about any complex areas in your copy that could be enhanced by using a metaphor.

- **Go For Short And Simple** - As with most elements of copy, the shorter and more concise you can make a metaphor, the greater the impact it will have.

- **Don't Overuse Them** - Use metaphors as much as you need them, but be careful not to stuff your copy with them because they're fun and demonstrate your creativity with words. Use them purposefully.

Related Searches:

list of metaphors

metaphor examples

popular metaphors

Remove Resistance

- **Be Indirect** - To neutralize resistance that most people have to a sales message, you must hand over control to them. Don't attempt to shove your message down their throat, but make your sales points indirectly.

- **Encourage Lots Of Small Yeses** - Subtly get your reader to answer 'yes' to simple statements and questions. These represent small, positive commitments in your readers minds - helps eliminate resistance and builds momentum to them saying 'yes' to your offer.

- **Provide Value Before Selling** - Give the reader something of value - teach them something - before even mentioning your product.

- **Wait To Display A Product Image** - Sometimes, an image of a product near the top of the page alerts the reader they're about to be sold - it may increase resistance.

- **Eliminate Confusion** - If at any step along the way of reading your copy the readers becomes confused, their resistance immediately gets stronger. You *must* keep your copy - from your headline to your order form - simple and easy to understand.

- **Back It Up** - The more you can prove that what you're saying is true (with facts, statistics, and testimonials), and that you know what you're talking about (by your reputation, results, and credentials), the more your reader will trust what you tell them.

- **Make It Urgent** - Using scarcity (deadlines for ordering, limited number of units, etc.) is one of the best, time-tested ways of moving people past any feeling of resistance into a state of taking action.

Answer Objections

- **Realize The Hidden Benefit Of Answering Objections** - Answering objections actually gives the reader ammo for defending their decision to buy.

- **Eliminate Objections ASAP** - By answering objections as soon as possible, you prevent doubt from festering in your reader's mind. The longer an objection stays in your reader's head, the more difficult it is to overcome.

- **Validate Their Feelings** - Be sure to validate your reader's skepticism: "You're right to wonder if this is a bunch of hype."

- **Provide An FAQ Section** - Simply make a list of all the objections your reader might have, and answer them succinctly one-by-one, like a series of FAQ's.

Related Searches:

create an faq page

- **Tell Them What It's Not** - Figure out all the negative things your reader might 'think' your product requires from them, then tell them it has nothing to do with those (include images with X's through them for bonus points):

  - It's NOT about selling to your friends and family

  - It's NOT about calling strangers

  - It's NOT about buying an inventory of products.

- **Tell Them Who's Benefiting From It Now** - To answer the common objection that people hear in their head, 'Is it for me?', answer with a breakdown of: Who loves/uses/relies on this product or service? For example, when writing about a course to stop a dog from barking, you would say:

> Who uses the **Bark-Stop** program?
>
> • Homeowners who are embarrassed that their pet is keeping their neighbors awake at night
>
> • Dog owners who are frustrated that having a peaceful, quiet evening at home is next to impossible
>
> • Parents who want a calm pet for their kids to play with without fear

- **Remember To Address These Common Objections** – The following list of objections are fairly common, no matter what your product is. Be sure your copy answers them:

> • **I don't have enough time; I'm in no hurry to act** - Demonstrate how easy it is to use, or do, maybe with a demo video. Explain to them clearly how much time they'll actually save.
>
> • **It's too much money; I don't have any money** - Show the reader what it will cost if they *don't* act. Or, show them the cost of other solutions (your competitor's products) that aren't as effective.
>
> • **It's similar to something they already have; I have no need for it** - Create a

comparison chart and compare your product to commonly used competing products and show how your product is different and better.

- **I have no interest in it; I don't think it's for me** - Remind them they won't know for sure until they try it, which they can do, risk-free, due to your fantastic money-back guarantee!

- **You've given me no proof that what you're saying is true; I don't trust you** - Offer case studies, testimonials, facts and statistics from reliable sources.

Related Searches:

comparison chart - <u>Images</u>

how to create a comparison chart - <u>Videos</u>

Show, Don't Just Tell

- **Back Up What You're Saying** - Case studies, links to relevant articles, testimonials, and stories can all be effective ways to show, and not just tell.

- **Include Lots Of Details** - Including plenty of details in your copy is like adding focus. Details help the reader see something vividly and clearly so that it becomes more real in their minds.

- **Use Images** - Display pictures of specific results that customers have achieved. Before and after photos work especially well.

- **Use Video** - Use video to show how easy something is to use, or how quickly results are produced.

Ask Questions

- **Understand Why Questions Are So Powerful** - Asking good questions in your copy:

  - Stimulates the reader's thinking, and gets them more emotionally involved in what you're saying.

  - Causes the reader to convince themselves something is true, instead of you simply making a statement, *expecting* them to believe it as true.

  - Leads your reader in a direction you want them to follow.

  - Solicits a response in your reader's mind, whether they know it or not. It's almost reflexive. They may not answer out loud, but they do in their mind.

  - Opens a 'loop' in the reader's brain that can only be closed by finding the answer. If left open, the person begins to feel a form of mental (and sometimes even physical) discomfort.

- **Value The Reader's Opinion** - Ask questions that show the reader you value their opinion: 'How would you...?', or 'What sounds more reasonable...?'

- **Ask Thought-Provoking Questions** - Use questions that arouse the reader's curiosity and gets them to think:

> - "How Did I Turn A $10 Website Into An Online Empire?"
>
> - "How Do You Know For Sure When Somebody is Lying To You?"

- **Remind Them Of Their Pain** - Ask questions that appeal to a pain:

> - "Are You Making These Kinds Of Mistakes With Your New Puppy?"
>
> - "Is All That 'Fat' Food That You Can't Stop Eating Putting You On A Guilt-Train You Desperately Want To Get Off?"

- **Go For A 'Yes!'** - Ask leading questions that require positive, 'yes' answers:

> - "Could you use more time?"
>
> - "Are you frustrated that you work hard all day and have very little to show for it?"
>
> - "Do you feel frustrated and overwhelmed?"

- **Always Provide The Answer** - When you ask a question, answer it soon afterward. Don't leave your reader hanging, without an answer - it'll break any concentration they have for reading your copy until they get an answer.

Watch The Length Of Your Copy

- **Write With Purpose In Mind, Not Length** - Write just enough copy to get your point across effectively - no more, no less.

- **Always Test Your Results** - There's no single answer to every question regarding the length of your copy. As with most things related to copywriting, always test!

Long Copy

- **Understand The Benefits Of Long Copy** - Writing long copy:

  - Gives you more opportunities to persuade the reader.

  - Appeals to both those who want to skim and those who want all their questions answered.

  - Usually helps your page rank better on search engines.

  - Tends to give the reader the impression that there must be something valuable about your offer if there's so much information about it (even if they don't read it all).

  - Helps you master the art of copywriting more quickly.

- **Know When To Use Long Copy** - Long copy is usually best when:

> - You're selling a high-priced product (more than $200.00).
>
> - A buying decision is based more on emotion (a course on running a home-based business) than practicality (a new pair of glasses).
>
> - Your product is ground-breaking, thus needs to be explained in greater detail
>
> - Your target market is unfamiliar with you or your product, and are likely to have a lot of questions that need answered.

Short Copy

- **Understand The Benefits Of Short Copy** - Writing short copy:

> - Makes your sales page look less like the 'hypey' long sales pages people are familiar with.
>
> - Motivates you to make better use of testimonials, bullets, audio, and video content.
>
> - May appeal to your market if they are known for being strapped for time (working mothers, time-management fans, etc.).

- **Know When To Use Short Copy** - Short copy is usually best when:

- You're product is inexpensive or free.

- You have a rock-solid reputation with your market of consistently delivering high-quality products.

- Everybody wants what you're selling.

Use Simplicity

- **Get To The Point Quickly** - Make sure it takes no more than 3-5 seconds to understand a point you make in your copy.

- **Edit For Simplicity** - Keep these elements simple:

  - **Headlines and subheadlines** - The shorter, the better

  - **Words** - Use words with similar meanings but fewer syllables

  - **Sentences** - Keep sentences short and free of unnecessary words

  - **Design** - Use just a few different colors, fonts, plenty of white space, and a simple page background

- **Study Twitter Posts** - Twitter (www.twitter.com) is a site that allows people to share their thoughts in 140 characters or less. It's a writing environment that requires simple, brief statements. Study some of the top posters to learn how they effectively get their thoughts across in a simple way.

  Related Searches:

  top tweeters

In A Nutshell: Things Your Copy Must Do!

Your copy *must*:

- Grab attention

- Focus on a single idea

- Be easy to scan

- Answer 'why', and 'what's in it for me?'

- Establish credibility and build trust in what you're saying

- Emphasize benefits, not features

- Clearly explain the uniqueness of the product - your USP (Unique Selling Proposition)

- Be written conversationally, using words and terms your reader is familiar with

- Address objections

- Provide a simple, clear message

- Convey massive value

- Reach the reader on an emotional level

- Create a sense of urgency

- Tell the reader what to do next

- Make it easy for them to take action

Copy
Elements

Headlines

- **Brainstorm Lots Of Ideas** - Spend a session doing nothing but writing down headline ideas. Write dozens, or even hundreds of headlines, before selecting one. Your headline represents 80% of your copy's success. Make sure you have the right one.

- **Be Truthful** - NEVER mislead the reader with your headline! You'll not only lose the sale, but worse...your reputation.

- **Always Focus On A Benefit** - You capture someone's attention by making a statement that expresses a unique benefit to them. Make clear, vivid benefits the highlight of your headlines.

- **Use Power Words** - Include words in your headlines such as:

  - Discover
  - Free
  - Easy
  - How To
  - Results
  - New
  - Proven
  - Quick
  - Why
  - Now
  - Announcing

- **Be Specific** - Be specific when using facts and figures in your headline.

- **Identify With Your Market** - When writing to mothers, mention the word, 'mothers,' somewhere in your headline.

- **Make It Red** - The purpose of your headline is to grab people's attention. Red is a color that demands to be noticed, and will help bring attention to your headline.

- **Put It In Quotes** - Statements placed in quotes ("") are perceived to have more authority behind them.

- **Center It** - When you center your headline on the page, it gives it visual position of importance.

- **Cap Your Words** - Begin each word in your headline with a capital letter. This makes each word appear important.

- **Avoid Using ALL CAPS** - Use both upper and lowercase letters.

- **Forget About Using A Period** - A period (.) indicates the end of a statement, and that the reader should prepare their mind for the next thought. You want them to think about your headline for a while, so don't include a period.

- **The Shorter, The Better** - Use shorter headlines. They're easier to understand, so they tend to have a greater impact!

- **Group Words Logically** - When using multi-line headlines, group the words on each line so they make sense on their own:

"Dance The Salsa

Related Searches:

headline tips - <u>Videos</u>

how to headlines - <u>Videos</u>

writing great headlines - <u>Videos</u>

headline ideas

Headline Formulas

- **Ask A Question** - Engage the reader's mind by asking them a question that requires a positive response:

> **"Are You Ready To Spend
> More Quality Time With Your Family,
> And Less Time At The Office?"**

- **Use A Testimonial** - Let your customers speak for you:

> **"I Never Thought I Could Play
> A Guitar Solo That Could Impress Anyone,
> But After 4 Standing Ovations,
> I'm Convinced!"**

- **Include Your Guarantee** - Back up the validity of your headline by incorporating your guarantee:

> **"In Less Than 30 Days,
> You'll Be Sleeping Better Than Your 5-Year Old,
> Or I'll Give You A Full Refund"**

- **Tie It To A Current News Item** - Associating your headline with something recently in the news adds credibility, freshness, and urgency to it:

> **"The Current Crisis In The Middle East
> Is About To Trigger An Explosive Green Energy Boon -
> Are You Ready For It?"**

- **Add A Time Element** - People want quick results. Include a time-limit in your headline ("10 minutes a day", "in just 7 days", etc.) to give them a tangible expectation of when they can expect results:

**"Discover The Secrets To
Typing Like An Executive Secretary
In Just 7 Days"**

- **Announce Something Big** - Let the reader know that something huge is on the horizon:

**"Announcing A Health Discovery
That May Put Your Dermatologist
Out Of Business"**

- **Enter The Conversation In Their Head** - Tap into the conversation your reader is having in their mind - why their problem is overwhelming them or keeping them awake at night:

**"Don't Let The Fear Of
How You're Going To Feed Your Family Next Week
Keep You Awake Any Longer"**

- **Make A Comparison** - Compare the specific results of your product with those of another:

**"The Super-Soaker Carpet Cleaner
Removes 30% More Dirt
Than Its Nearest Competitor"**

- **Tell A Story** - Connect with the reader right away by sharing an attention-grabbing part of a story:

**"Last Year, I Went From Being $137,219.32 In Debt,
To Owning My Home, Free And Clear -
Let Me Tell You The Secret To How I Did It"**

- Give A Command - Simply tell your reader what to do:

**"Reach Into Your Back Pocket,
Open Your Wallet,**

And Tell Me Whether It's As Full
As You Want It To Be"

- **Make A Recommendation** - Share your expertise:

**"The 3 Best Ways To Take Control
Of An Out-Of-Control Dog"**

- **Share A How To** - Promise to teach the reader something actionable they can use immediately:

**"How To Squeeze More Productivity
From Every Hour Of Your Day"**

- **Use Statistics** - Use relevant facts and figures to make a shocking revelation:

**"This Year Alone,
More Than 1.2 Million People
Will Lose Their Home -
Will You Be One Of Them"**

- **Offer Something Of Value** - Give something valuable away for free:

**"Grab This FREE Special Report,
And Discover How To Cut Your Taxes By 1/3 -
Even While Making More Money"**

Related Searches:

headline formulas

headline swipe file

Openings/Leads

- **Get Attention, Right Away** - Throw the best you've got at the reader, right out of the gate. Make the lead so magnetic, shocking, or emotionally charged, that it sets the tone for what the reader can expect from reading the rest of your copy:

> - **Debunk a commonly held belief** - "Your doctor probably has no idea how to cure your ongoing headaches."
>
> - **Make a prediction** - "3 years from now, nearly everyone on the planet will be affected with what I'm going to reveal to you right now."
>
> - **Provide some relevant facts and figures** - "Last year, more than 247,367 people lost their jobs because they didn't have this easy-to-learn skill"
>
> - **Tell a story** - "I'll never forget the day I walked into the kitchen to tell my wife we were loosing our home."
>
> - **State your offer** - "I want to show you how to get more done in a single day than most people get done in a week, using a simple 3-step system you can begin using today!"
>
> - **Make a promise** - "By the time you're done reading this page, you'll know how to stop your dog from barking on command, every single

time!"

- **Ask a question** - "Have you ever wondered why your credit card debt seems to never go away, despite paying faithfully for years and years?"

- **Share a secret** - "I'm about to reveal something to you that has enabled me to make a 6-figure income for the last 4 years, working only 15 hours a week."

- **Follow The Flow** - Write your lead so that what you say flows smoothly from what you said in your headline.

- **Get To The Point** - Your reader isn't interested in small talk, so don't waste any time getting to the point with your opening.

- **Maintain Focus On The Reader** - You want to include the word 'you' in your lead, as well as focus on the main emotional benefit your product offers to the reader.

- **Use Specific Salutations** - Don't say 'Dear Sir', but 'Dear Fellow Scrapbooker.' Use of the word 'Fellow' creates an instant connection between you and the reader; they're reading something from someone who does what they do.

- **Use A Drop Cap** - Make the first letter of your lead a drop cap (a very large letter). This is a great way to draw the readers eye to your lead.

Related Searches:

drop caps - Images

Subheadlines

- **Make Your Copy Digestible** - Use subheads as often as possible, they make your copy easier to scan and read. No only that, but they give you more opportunities to catch the reader's attention with a statement that could pull them deeper into your copy, increasing your chances of getting them to take action!

- **Tell A Story** - Review your subheads to make sure that when read, one after the other, they tell the complete story of your sales letter.

- **Tie Them To Your Main Benefit** - Subheadlines should be related to the main benefit of your product or service.

- **Keep Them Relevant** - A subhead should be directly related to the content that follows it.

- **Don't Skimp** - Subheads should be strong enough to be used as headlines, and should stir the reader's curiosity to read more.

- **Learn To Recycle** - A great source for subheadline ideas are your discarded main headline ideas.

Bullets

- **Focus On Benefits** - Each bullet must contain a benefit. It should solicit a response in the readers mind of, 'Yes, that would be nice!'

- **Answer A 'Why'** - People need reasons 'why' in order to feel compelled to take action. Use bullets to provide plenty of clear, concise, simple reasons why they should take action!

- **Use Blind Bullets** - Give just enough information in the bullet to leave the reader curious to know the answer. For example:

- **Make Them Visually Appealing** - Alternate the styling of individual bullets in a group - it's easier on the eyes:

  - **Bold**

  - Unbold

  - **Bold**

  - Unbold

- **Use Plenty Of White Space** - Include enough white space between bullets to make them easy to scan.

- **Spice Them Up With Graphics** - Use a checkmark image or some other colorful graphic to make your bullets stand out even more.

- **Keep Them Short** - It's best to keep each bullet point to no more than 3 lines each. If you go any longer, you begin to defeat the purpose of using bullets in the first place - scalability.

- **Use Bullets Generously** - Include several sections of bullets in your copy. They're a great way to break up long blocks of text, and each section 'piles on the value' of your product in the readers' eyes.

- **List Your Bullets Strategically** - List bullets in order of importance as follows:

  - The most important benefit

  - The second most important benefit

  - Less important point

  - Less important point

  - Third most important benefit

- **Front-Load Your Bullets** - Put important keywords or phrases at the beginning of each bullet.

- **Strive For Symmetry** - Keep your bullets symmetrical when possible; Keep them all just 1 line, 2 lines, or 3 lines.

- **Look To Amazon For Inspiration** - Need ideas for bullets? Go to Amazon.com and review the table of contents of some of the most popular books in your niche. Each item is a potential bullet!

General Styling

- **Use Formatting To Your Advantage** - Formatting of various elements in your copy should be done to emphasize key points. But don't overdo it, because when everything is special, then nothing is!

- **Use Fonts Creatively** - Using various fonts for different elements makes them stand out better, but avoid using too many fonts, which can make your copy look like a ransom note.

- **Add Some Excitement** - Italics, underlining, bolding, and ALL CAPS add excitement to your writing.

- **Format To Tell A Hidden Story** - When read in order, bolded, italicized, and underlined words should tell their own story - in and of themselves - without the need for the surrounding text.

- **Highlight In A Familiar Way** - Use yellow highlighting to emphasize key words or phrases, but use it sparingly.

- **Use White Space Generously** - Use plenty of white space, it makes your copy easier read and understand.

- **Keep Columns Narrow** - Wide columns of text require the reader's eyes to move a greater distance to leave the end of one line of text and begin the next. Narrower columns help reduce fatigue from this eye movement.

- **Stick With Standard Fonts** - Use easy-to-read fonts such as Times New Roman, `Courier New`, or Arial (for the Web).

- **Don't Do Reverse** - Avoid reverse type, or light-colored text against a dark background. It's harder to read than black text on a white background.

Graphics & Photos

- **Keep Graphics In Their Place** - Words sell - graphics and images simply support the words.

- **Let Them See What They Get** - Include images of your product. Be sure to include images of everything that comes with your offer (every last book, tip sheet, CD, workbook - everything).

- **Don't Reveal Too Soon** - Avoid showing images of your product early in your copy. It may alert your reader they're about to be sold, causing them to move on to something else. Sell them emotionally first.

- **Show Them The Interface** - If you're selling software, include screenshots of the interface.

  Related Searches:

  screenshots software

  screenshot software reviews

  how to take a screenshot - Videos

- **Tap Into The Human Connection** - Whenever possible, use pictures of human beings instead of objects - people connect with people.

- **Show People Experiencing The Result** - When using pictures of people, make sure they represent the image you want your reader to identify with while, or after, using the product or service.

- **Show The Creator In Action** - Use an image of the creator/author of the product. Action shots (like those of the person speaking or answering questions at a seminar) work better than studio shots.

- **Visually Demonstrate The Main Benefit** - Use an image that represents the main benefit of the product or service. If the main benefit is more time, show an image of a person playing with their kids, or working on a hobby.

- **Use Images To Lead The Reader's Eyes** - Make sure that elements in the photo point in the direction you want to lead your readers. For example, people facing toward the right of the photo will lead your readers that way, perhaps to an important headline.

- **Show Before & After Results** - Where applicable, use before and after shots - indicate that they are original, untouched, unaltered images (make sure they are).

- **Give Younger Readers More Visuals** - Use more graphics when appealing to a younger market. They're used to more visual elements and tend to become quickly uninterested in the absence of them.

- **Add Some Doodles** - Include 'hand-written' notes and symbols (stars, circles, etc.) in the margins of your copy to make certain points stand out, and make it feel more personal.

  Related Searches:

  copy doodles

- **Use Attention-Grabbing Photos** - The best attention-grabbing photos include:

  - Babies
  - A pretty girl

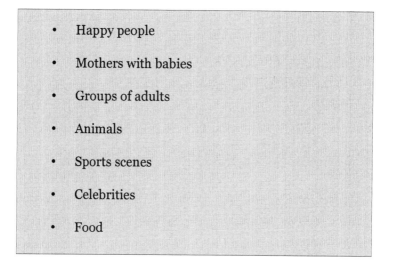

- Happy people

- Mothers with babies

- Groups of adults

- Animals

- Sports scenes

- Celebrities

- Food

Related Searches:

stock photos

free stock photos

photo editor

online photo editor

Proof

- **Remember Why You Need Proof** - Proof is less about you convincing the reader, and more about the reader convincing themselves, which is way more effective. Proof enhances the trust the reader has in what you say.

- **Be Specific** - Use as many details and as much specificity in your proof as possible.

- **Front-Load Your Proof** - Put your most compelling proof towards the top of your copy.

- **Be Honest** - It should go without saying that your proof must always be truthful and real. NEVER make it up!

- **Keep It Legal** - The U.S. Federal Trade Commission provides a set of guidelines that you must follow when using testimonials, endorsements, and other forms of proof. Either run your proof by an attorney, or research the guidelines yourself with the following searches.

  Related Searches:

  new ftc guidelines - <u>Videos</u>

  ftc testimonial | endorsement guidelines

Testimonials

- **Remember Why Testimonials Work** - People are often persuaded by their peers.

- **Loose The Hype** - Although you can't control what your customers say, it's best if they can provide an honest review of their experience with your product without using hypey words such as, 'amazing', 'mind-blowing', or 'incredible.' These kinds of words make your testimonials sound less sincere.

- **Focus On Results** - Use testimonials that discuss the achievement of the desired result of the product. Avoid irrelevant or general testimonials.

- **Place Testimonials With A Purpose** - Use these guidelines when placing testimonials on the page:

  - Place testimonials that discuss a specific benefit somewhere close to where that benefit is discussed in the copy.

  - Place a large chunk of testimonials at the end of your copy. Be sure to include your call to action after the last testimonial.

  - Place testimonials in a column along the right side of the page.

- **Go For Quality Over Quantity** - A few quality testimonials are worth more than 10 testimonials that are vague and hypey.

- **Use A Headline** - Begin each testimonial with a headline, which should be a quote from the customer that highlights their positive results.

- **Include Plenty Of Details** - When possible, include a picture, signature, full name, Website, and the title/position of the customer. Remember specificity promotes trust in you and your message.

- **Don't Over-Produce Images** - When including images with testimonials, make sure they don't look too produced (perfect color, sharpness, a studio background, etc.), as these tend to look less authentic than somewhat blurry, 'at-home' photos.

- **Use Video** - Ask your customers to record a short video testimonial (YouTube has a feature that allows them to do this). When using video testimonials, never set them to autoplay.

Related Searches:

youtube quickcapture - <u>Videos</u>

- **Get The Best You Can** - Audio testimonials are usually better than text, and video is usually better than audio. Once again, the more human you can make your testimonials, the better.

- **Use Creative Ways To Get Testimonials** - Use these ideas to grow your file of testimonials:

> - Provide a testimonial page or form on your site. Provide a link to this page in your products and emails.
>
> - If you use an autoresponder, include a message in your sequence that asks for a testimonial or feedback. Provide a link to your testimonial page.
>
> - When asking for a testimonial, make it clear that you value your customer's opinion. People love offering their opinion.
>
> - Timing is everything; Ask for testimonials just after you wow the customer, such as at the end of a seminar, a course, or after answering a question for them.

- Get video testimonials after you speak at an event, or take a camera to your client and ask for a brief testimonial.

- When writing for a client, ask them for any testimonials they have.

Related Searches:

getting | acquiring testimonials - Videos

testimonial tips

Other Forms Of Proof

- **Obtain Endorsements** - Do what you can to obtain endorsements for your product from:

  - Industry experts

  - Professionals in the field

  - Celebrities

- **Put Your Credentials To Work** - Answers the question of 'why should I listen to you?':

  - List any awards, affiliations, and accomplishments.

  - Use your age, experience, and years in business.

  - Mention the titles of any books authored.

- List certifications. Include the name of schools and/or any distinguished or recognizable instructors.

- Include a well-crafted bio.

- Emphasize how you are not a know-it-all, but instead how you're really, really good at achieving the result the reader wants.

- **Share Your Track Record** - Prove to your readers that you and your product have a great history of results:

  - Provide case studies of your best students' results (in the form of a report, or an audio/video interview).

  - State the number of customers you have served.

  - State the number of products you have sold.

  - State the number of years your product has been around.

- **Use Media To Your Advantage** – Include:

  - Screenshots of earnings, checks, and bank statements.

  - Charts and graphs. Even if the reader doesn't completely understand them (hopefully they do), it still adds a look of credibility.

- Before and after shots.

- Video demos.

- Newspaper clippings and write ups from authoritative resources. Use logos where possible.

- Photos of events (especially if you're a speaker).

- **Get Others To Back You Up** - Use relevant 3rd-party data:

  - Find government reports that back up your claims.

  - Provide technical data and statistics that back up your claims.

- **Transfer Credibility** - Use graphics, symbols, and when possible, logos, on your sales page that the reader already considers credible. This subtly 'transfers' that credibility to your product.

Bonuses & Premiums

- **Be Creative** - Bonuses and premiums can be information products (such as reports, tip sheets, forms, etc.), or physical products (such as a CD, DVD, or book).

- **Turn A Promise Into A Bonus** - One of the best bonuses is to take one or two of your product's smaller promises or benefits and turn those into special reports.

- **Provide Real Value** - Each bonus should be valuable enough that the reader would buy it based on its own merit.

- **Indicate The Value** - Include the value of the bonus next to the description of the bonus. Be specific with the amount you show.

- **Show A Rundown** - When offering multiple bonuses, display a summary rundown containing the value of each bonus item, with a total at the bottom.

- **Make Your Bonuses Tangible** - Include an image of each bonus to make it more real to your reader. Use virtual covers and boxes for digital products.

  Related Searches:

  ebook cover - Videos

  ebook cover photoshop action

  ecover software - Videos

- **Avoid Bonus Overload** - Too many bonuses can:

  - Confuse the reader and take their focus off your

main product.

- Make buyers suspicious that the bonuses are being used to deflect from a lack of quality in the main product.

- Result in more refunds, as they tend to push the reader to buy when they wouldn't have otherwise, thus it's easier for them to regret their decision later.

- **Let Luxury Stand On Its Own** - Bonuses can diminish the perceived value of expensive or luxury items. If the product or service is truly elite and desirable, the addition of a bonus can seem suspicious or cheap.

Guarantees

- **Make It Longer** - The longer your guarantee (time-wise), the more sales you'll likely get.

- **Put It Where It They Can See It** - Don't try to hide or minimize your guarantee, which gives the impression you're afraid someone might see it and actually use it. Make it totally obvious, showing your reader you're confident enough in your product to offer the guarantee.

- **Sign It** - Most people tend to give more credibility to anything that contains a signature. Use this to your advantage by including your signature inside your guarantee.

- **Seal It** - Include a seal graphic with your guarantee, which will give it a higher perceived importance and validity.

  Related Searches:

  guarantee seal - Images

- **Write It Out** - Write out your guarantee by hand (use blue ink). This will humanize it more and add a layer of trust.

- **Let Them Keep The Bonuses** - Indicate that the reader can keep the valuable bonuses, even if they choose to ask for a refund. Be sure to restate the value of bonuses in specific monetary terms.

- **Lose The Legalese** - Make your guarantee easy to read and understand by editing out any hard-to-understand legalese. Remember, if it's confusing, or looks too legal, it will probably raise your reader's resistance to your offer.

- **Use A Multi-Guarantee** - Break up elements of your guarantee into a set of bullet points, which will give it more of an overall perceived value. Name the bullets *Guarantee 1*, *Guarantee 2*, etc.

- **Do A Video** - Create a video-based guarantee, where you share the content of the guarantee with the reader, face-to-face. This increases the believability of what you promise.

- **Avoid Using Multiple-Your-Money-back Guarantees** - These kinds of guarantees sound too desperate and hypey. A legitimate product can stand on its own with a standard money-back guarantee.

- **Don't Promise Specific Results** - Promising specific results is not only impossible to do, but in some places, it's illegal. So don't do it!

- **Do A Legal Check** - Run your guarantee by the legal department (if you have one), or have your attorney review it. You don't want to promise something that might get you in hot water sometime later.

- **Test It** - Include your guarantee in any split-testing you do on your copy.

- **Use These Powerful Phrases** - Include these time-tested phrases somewhere in your guarantee copy:

  - "prompt and courteous refund"

  - "no hassles, no questions asked, no hard feelings refund"

  - "no questions asked"

  - "Better-Than-Risk-Free"

  - "You Can't Lose!"

- "Unconditional, Money-Back Guarantee"

- "Your Money Back, No Questions Asked"

- "I Personally Guarantee"

- "No Way That You Can Lose"

- "30-Day Free Examination"

- "Iron-Clad Money-Back Guarantee"

- "100% On-The-Spot Full Refund"

- "Absolutely No Risk To You!"

- "100%, no-hassle refund!"

Order/Call To Action

- **Don't Apologize** - Never come across apologetic when stating your offer. Be clear, to-the-point, and confident that what you have to offer is something of immense value.

- **Tell Them Specifically What To Do** - Give clear, specific directions for ordering and receiving of goods, even a simple step-by-step guide of the process. Tell your reader what to do!

- **Let Them Know What To Expect** - Tell the purchaser when they will receive the product, and in what form.

Scarcity

- **Use Scarcity** - The reader must be given a compelling reason to order right now - this very moment! Use one of these scarcity strategies:

    - **Limited copies** - Limit the number of units that are for sale. On the Web, show a dynamically updated number of units that are still available, and cross-out the original number.

    - **Limited time** - Explain that the offer will be removed, or the price increased, after a certain time-limit has passed. On the Web, include a countdown timer with a warning symbol (a graphic), with the words: "This Offer Ends In XX:XX (days, hours, or minutes)."

    Related Searches:

javascript countdown

- **Limited guarantee** - Offer a longer or better guarantee for people who purchase within a certain time frame, or who are among the first 500 customers.

- **Limited bonuses or premiums** - Remove certain bonuses or premiums after a number of units have sold, or time has passed. This is especially effective when the premiums come from a third party, as you have no control as to when that 3rd-party will want their bonus(es) removed.

- **Limited price** - Let the reader know that the price will go up after the initial product marketing 'testing.'

- **Limited extras** - Offer free shipping, support, or installation for a limited time, or units sold.

- **Be Honest About Your Claims** - Never use untruthful tactics when implementing scarcity. Be true to your deadlines, number of copies, etc.

- **Tell Them Why** - Provide a reason why only a limited time or number of products are available. Giving a valid reason instills trust, and lets your reader know that you're not just 'blowing smoke.'

Related Searches:

scarcity copywriting

scarcity principle

psychology of scarcity

Order Form

- **Assume The Sale** - Include elements that assume the reader is sold:

    - Start the order form with the word "Yes!", followed by the promise of your offer: "Yes! I'm ready to squeeze more time out of every day." This creates the assumption that the reader is consenting to your offer.

    - Include a checkbox and make it appear already checked.

    - Include 2 or 3 of your most important benefits in your order form. Use the voice of the reader: "I want to learn the 5 easiest ways to lose weight eating chocolate." Or, "I want to take advantage of your lifetime guarantee!"

- **Avoid Negative Associations** - Never use the words 'Order' or 'Form' to describe your order form. These words typically have negative associations in most readers' minds. Call it a 'Risk-Free Acceptance Certificate.'

- **Label Your Order Button Correctly** - Use the phrase 'Add To Cart', as the text for your order button. This works much better than 'Order Now.'

- **Make It Inviting** - Make your order form graphically pleasing.

Include an image of your product, or of smiling people. Surround it with a certificate-looking border, or dash border.

- **Show Them What You Accept** - Include images of the forms of payment you accept, such as credit cards, eCheck, etc.

- **Provide Some Peace Of Mind** - Indicate that the ordering process is secure (make sure it us). For better results, include a lock graphic, or something similar, to denote the idea of security.

- **Keep It Simple** - Your order form should be uncluttered, clean, and easy to follow.

Price

- **Use A Slam-Dunk Approach** - Convince your reader to accept the value of a higher price, then BAM!...offer them a discount.

- **Visually Cancel-Out Higher Prices** - Use a strike-through on a high price when offering a discounted price.

- **Avoid Percentage Discounts** - When stating a discount, avoid using percentages (40% off). Readers don't do math! State the discount as a figure ($27.13).

- **Explain Your Discount** - Always provide a reason for a discounted price. Otherwise, it simply looks like meaningless marketing fluff.

- **Use Supermarket Pricing** - Use prices that end prices in 7 (27.77 - 49.97). This indicates your attention to detail and conveys the idea that you're not asking for a cent more than your product or service is worth.

- **Use Prestige Pricing** - For high-end products, use prestige pricing, or a price that ends in a round number ($1000.00 instead of $997.00). This indicates that your product is less about value and more about top-quality results.

- **Price Your Product Based On Its Value** - Price isn't dependent on the physical size of your product, but the value of its content to the customer.

- **Amortize The Cost** - Split your price down to number of uses: "If you grab my product for $47.77 and use it 100 times, that's just 47 cents per use. That's much less than the $200 per hour you'd pay a professional."

- **Explain The Savings** - Explain how much money the reader is saving by using your product.

- **Make The Value Of The Product Clear** - Justify the price by providing details into the development of your product, and what it would cost the reader to have something similar created themselves.

- **Explain The Cost Of Inaction** - Make it clear to your reader what it will cost them (in time and money) if they don't order your product right now.

- **Provide A Point Of Reference** - Share with your reader the price others have paid for your product in the past.

Related Searches:

how to price a product - Videos

product pricing strategy - Videos

Signature

- **Add A Signature To Your Copy** - Include your signature with all your copy. It's a way of showing the reader your approval of what has been written - you're willing to attach your name and reputation to it!

- **Go Blue** - If possible, use a blue 'ink' version of your signature. It looks more authentic and less like it came off a 'copy machine.'

- **Provide A Printed Version** - Include your typed/printed name after the signature graphic. This makes your copy look more professional.

Related Searches:

scan your signature

P.S.

- **Realize Their Power** - The P.S. is typically the 2nd most-read part of your copy, after your headline.

- **Go Easy On Them** - Avoid using too many P.S.'s. It will diminish their value and impact.

- **Use Them Creatively** - Use a P.S. To:

  - Review your offer

  - Restate your guarantee

  - Restate your product's ultimate benefit

  - Include a case study

  - Answer FAQs

  - Provide a video

Contact & Support

- **Provide Several Clear Points Of Contact** - Provide clear information for how the reader can reach you for support - a personal email address (not info@ or support@ or webmaster@), phone number, address, URL, etc.

- **Be Informative** - Provide a Contact page that includes a mailing address and phone number, as well as photos and bios of you and your staff. This shows customers they're doing business with real people.

- **Don't Abbreviate** - Avoid abbreviations in contact details as they may not be understood by everyone, especially those in other countries.

- **Respond Quickly** - Answer emails and voicemails quickly (24 hours or less). Not only will the people who contact you appreciate it, but it helps eliminate stress from your life.

- **Motivate The Reader To Contact You** - When providing a URL or phone number, provide the reader a reason to contact you. Offer them a free report, tips, a complimentary subscription to your newsletter, etc.

- **Be Social** - If you use Twitter or Facebook, provide links to these pages as well.

Related Searches:

social marketing - Videos

social marketing tips - Videos

twitter tips - Videos

twitter marketing tips - <u>Videos</u>

facebook tips - <u>Videos</u>

facebook marketing tips - <u>Videos</u>

Related Searches:

contact page tips

Disclaimers

- **Protect Yourself** - Provide links in your copy to all of these:

Privacy Statement

Related Searches:

privacy statement example

privacy statement template

privacy statement generator

Earnings Disclaimer

Related Searches:

privacy statement template

privacy statement generator

Terms Of Use

Related Searches:

privacy statement template

privacy statement generator

Web
Copywriting

General Web Copywriting

- **Do A Speed Check** - Make sure your pages load fast. Even in a world full of high-speed Internet connections, this is important.

  Related Searches:

  page load speed checker

- **Do A Browser Check** - Test how your sales page looks in multiple browsers. Use *Adobe's BrowserLab* (search *Google* for *adobe browserlab*) for an automated way of doing this.

- **Keep It Clean & Simple** - Keep your navigation simple, intuitive, and consistent across all pages.

- **Explain Your Privacy Terms** - Always include a privacy statement next to any forms that ask the reader for their name or email address. Explain how you use the info, whether it's shared with 3rd- party vendors, and how they can opt-out if they choose to do so.

  Related Searches:

  privacy statement template

  privacy statement generator

- **Make Your Pages Print-Friendly** - Offer a Print button at the top of your sales page, and make sure it creates a good-looking result.

  Related Searches:

  how to create a print page button

SEO (Search Engine Optimization)

Keywords

- **Be Very Specific** - Optimize your Web pages using long-tail keywords related to the content of the page:

> Not *vitamins* but, *organic vitamins for kids*

Related Searches:

long tail keywords - <u>Videos</u>

what are long tail keywords - <u>Videos</u>

- **Understand Why You Should Use Long-tail Keywords** - The benefits of targeting long-tail keywords include:

  - Searchers who use them are closer to making a buying decision.

  - There's less competition for these kinds of keywords, so there's a greater chance of you standing out in the search engines.

  - You still get traffic from broad searches that contain any of your long-tail keywords, so you get the best of both worlds!

- **Target Both Singular & Plural Forms** - Write copy that uses both singular and plural forms of keywords:

> - **Example 1:** "Organic *vitamins* for kids are great..."
> - **Example 2:** "If you give an organic *vitamin* to a kid..."

- **Use Related Words & Synonyms** - It's a good idea to include variations of your keywords in your copy:

> - *samples* AND *examples*
> - *keyword frequency* AND *keyword density*

- **Think Like Your Visitor** - Use keywords that reflect the thinking of your visitor when they search for an answer:

> - Not *turkey cooking tips* but, *how do I cook a turkey*

- **Optimize Individual Pages** - Each page on a site can be a unique traffic generator. Always optimize individual pages for specific long-tail keywords.

- **Include Keywords In Links** - Use relevant keywords within links (the text that describes where the links takes the visitor when it's clicked).

- **Don't Forget ALT Tags** - Use keywords in ALT tags to describe the content of images (which are used for when the reader has the display of images on a Web page disabled).

- **Use These Keyword Frequency Guidelines** - Include keywords on your pages using the following guidelines as a general rule:

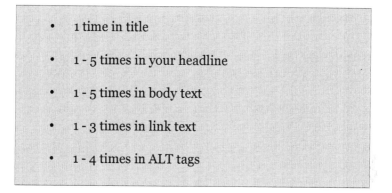

- 1 time in title

- 1 - 5 times in your headline

- 1 - 5 times in body text

- 1 - 3 times in link text

- 1 - 4 times in ALT tags

Related Searches:

seo keyword density | frequency

seo keyword best practices

Domain Names

Choose A Great Domain Name - The domain you choose should:

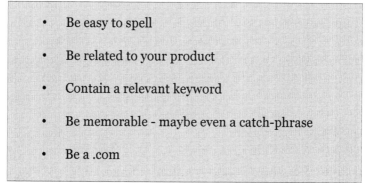

- Be easy to spell

- Be related to your product

- Contain a relevant keyword

- Be memorable - maybe even a catch-phrase

- Be a .com

choose | choosing a domain name - <u>Videos</u>

domain name tips - <u>Videos</u>

domain name search

Page Titles

- **Optimize Your Page Titles** - Remember that the titles of your Web pages (within the HTML <title> tag):

  - Should be as short as possible

  - Should be accurate - correctly describing the content of the page it's associated with

  - Should contain relevant keywords, which should be as close to the beginning of the page title as possible

  - Should be unique for each page of your site

  - Should contain a call to action (like a headline)

  - Should be as similar to your headline as possible

  - Should not be stuffed with keywords

  - Are very important in the eyes of most search engines

Meta Tags

- **Optimize Your Meta Tags** – Use the following guidelines to optimize your meta tags:

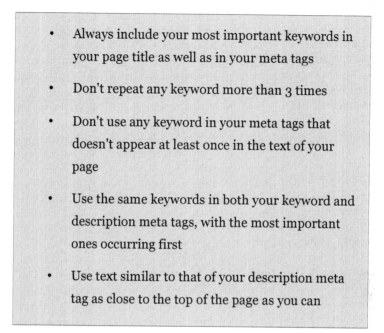

- Always include your most important keywords in your page title as well as in your meta tags

- Don't repeat any keyword more than 3 times

- Don't use any keyword in your meta tags that doesn't appear at least once in the text of your page

- Use the same keywords in both your keyword and description meta tags, with the most important ones occurring first

- Use text similar to that of your description meta tag as close to the top of the page as you can

Related Searches:

optimize meta tags - <u>Videos</u>

Headlines

- **Optimize For The Long-Tail** - Use long-tail keywords in your headline. It improves your SEO, and it appears in search results for people to read.

- **Use The Right HTML Tags** - Style your headline using an <h1> tag, not simply by using a big font. Search engines give more weight to the content within <h1> tags. Use <h2> tags for subheadlines and other text elements that incorporate important keywords.

- **Stick It At The Very Top** - Put your headline at the very top of your page - before images, or any other text.

Links

- **Give Thought To Your Links** - Make your text links relevant and descriptive. If you have link to a page about a weight loss tips, write a link that says something like, "Get weight loss tips."

Related Searches:

seo tips - Videos

seo tricks - Videos

link building - Videos

link building tips - Videos

link building strategies - Videos

web traffic tips - Videos

increase web traffic - Videos

Media: General

- **Remember The Benefits Of Using Media** - Different forms of media brings personality to a sales page. In addition, audio and video content helps readers connect with you on a deeper level.

- **Use Audio & Video Content For These Elements** – Consider using media, like audio and video, in the following areas of your copy:

  - **Testimonials** - Ask satisfied customers to record a short audio or video clip with them sharing their experience with your product or service.

  - **Introductions** - Include an introductory video at the top of your sales page. Share a 'preview' of your sales letter, highlighting some of the content in your headlines and bullet points.

  - **Opt-in box** - Personally invite readers to sign-up for your newsletter, free report, or whatever other incentive you're using to capture their email address. Always explain the value and benefits of opting in.

  - **Bonus gifts** - Provide mini-previews of each bonus item you include with your offer. Relate the value of the bonus, and all the benefits of having and using it.

  - **Guarantee** - Add some credibility to your guarantee by looking the viewer in the eye and telling them exactly how you stand behind your offer.

- **Order pages** - Provide clear instructions on how to order, and what happens at the end of the ordering process (such as how they'll receive the product).

- **Thank You pages** - Include a video on a thank you page to express your thanks for their order, or to offer an upsell of some sort.

Media: Audio

- **Remember The Benefit Of Using It** - Using audio adds credibility to your message, and usually helps generate a higher response.

- **Test Adding A Picture** - Test whether adding a picture of yourself next to an audio player improves the page's conversion.

- **Keep It Short** - Audio on a sales page should be less than 5 minutes in length.

- **Know Your Outcome** - The purpose of your audio should be to either introduce yourself, or get your visitor to take an action.

- **Be Enthusiastic & Natural** - When recording your audio, be sure to stand up, use gestures, and speak conversationally - avoid reading a script verbatim.

- **Be Considerate Of Corporate Customers** - Audio may not be feasible to corporate customers who may not have speakers attached to their computers or who don't want to be 'caught' by their bosses doing something other than work.

- **Do What's Expected** - Only autoplay audio when the user is expecting to hear audio.

- **Speak Up For Yourself** - Use your own voice for most tasks, even if you don't feel you're the best communicator. It creates a valuable, authentic social connection with the listener.

- **Hire A Voice** - Consider using a professional voice talent when selling to the corporate market.

Related Searches:

voice talent | over

- **Use Front And Back Music** - Add a short music clip to the beginning and end of your audio clips. Fade them out when you begin to speak and fade them in as you're wrapping things up. This adds a bit of professionalism to any recording.

Related Searches:

royalty free music - Shopping

- **Go With A Headset Mic** - Use a quality headset microphone when recording audio. This will help eliminate background noise, and maintain a constant recording level, so that volume levels don't go up and down as you move your head.

Related Searches:

headset microphone - Shopping

headset microphone reviews - Videos

Related Searches:

home vocal recording tips - Videos

audio editor

free audio editor

audio editor online

how to record audio - Videos

Media : Video

- **Don't Create A Distraction** - Keep the background in your video simple. You don't want it to be a distraction in any way.

  Related Searches:

  video backgrounds - Shopping

  video backdrops - Shopping

- **Dress To Connect** - Dress in a way that connects with your audience. If you're selling to Everyday Joe's, dress like one. If you're selling to professionals, dress like one.

- **Be Natural** - People can easily detect phoniness, especially in a video. If you try come across as a professional speaker, when you're really a 'home-hermit', it'll do you more harm than good. Of course, be professional in what you say and do, but also, be who you are to your friends - natural.

- **Stay Under 3** - Keep your videos short, under three minutes, where possible. That's enough time to share something of value without losing the interest of your viewer.

- **Remain Eye-To-Eye** - Keep the video at eye-level or higher. *Never* record a video so that it appears you're looking down on your viewer.

- **Give People A Reason To Play** - Encourage viewers to watch your video. Include a teaser about the content of the video above the video window. Give viewers plenty of reasons to click the *Play* button!

- **Break Up Long Videos** - If you have a lot of video content you'd like to share, break it into separate videos. Include a subhead and bullets that highlight the content of each video.

- **Use A Watermark** - Always use watermark in your videos to display the URL of the site the video promotes.

- **Provide Value** - If you're going to ask someone to give you some of their time to watch your video, you need to give them something in return for doing so - value. While it's OK to use video for promoting things, you always want to provide value first - a tip, a recommendation, etc.

- **Avoid Rambling** - Very few people can press the *Record* button on a video camera and without preparation of any kind, create a compelling result. Establish the purpose of your video before you begin recording, create a simple outline, and practice a couple times. And whatever you do, don't just read a script - it's comes across way too insincere (because it is).

- **Include A Call To Action** - Just like written copy, your sales videos *must* include a call to action for the viewer.

- **Get Your Videos Seen** - Distribute your videos on the Web using a service like www.tubemogul.com, which will automatically submit them to multiple video-sharing sites. If you're willing to pay a monthly fee for a great distribution service, check out www.trafficgeyser.com.

Related Web Searches:

video marketing tips - <u>Videos</u>

how to create a viral video - <u>Videos</u>

viral videos - <u>Videos</u>

video camera - <u>Shopping</u>

video camera review - <u>Videos</u>

video editing software - <u>Shopping</u>

free video editing software

video editing software review - <u>Videos</u>

video editing tips - <u>Videos</u>

video editing tutorials - <u>Videos</u>

movie maker tutorials - <u>Videos</u>

imovie tutorials - <u>Videos</u>

After
You Write

Review Your Copy

- **Come Back To It With Fresh Eyes** - Put away your copy and don't look at it or think about it for a couple of days. Take a break from it before doing another review. You'll be amazed at how this will allow you to see your copy from a totally new perspective.

- **Spell Check** - Do a complete spell check of your copy before passing it off to your client for a review. While there's no avoiding some spelling errors, more than a few will not set well with most clients.

- **Hire A Proofreader** - To ensure you deliver as error-free copy as possible, hire a professional proofreader to review it.

  Related Searches:

  proofreading services

  proofreading tips

- **Review Your Copy In Reverse, From Finish To Start** - Read your copy backwards, from the last sentence to the first. You'll discover errors you wouldn't have seen otherwise.

- **Cut The Boring Parts** - Don't be afraid to remove chunks of your copy because they now sound boring to you.

- **Read It Out Loud** - Read your copy out loud, in a normal speaking voice. This helps you discover unnatural or odd-sounding sections of your copy. Make sure it sounds conversational.

- **Do Some Simple Real-World Testing** - Get a second opinion about your copy before sending it out. A trusted colleague is best, but your spouse's input can be valuable as well.

- **Review A Hard Copy** - Print your copy and go through it with a red marker. Highlight points that are boring, awkward, or break its flow.

- **Pay Attention To Small Details** - Remove unnecessary words, phrases, and sentences. If something doesn't contribute to the core of your message, then remove it!

- **Cut The Fluff** - Eliminate words like 'very', 'really', 'actually', and 'extremely.'

- **Check Your Copy For Readability** - Run your copy through a *Flesch-Kincaid* readability calculator (Microsoft Word has a built-in tool for this, or search *Google* for *readability calculator*). Shoot for a high reading-ease score, and a grade-level of 7.5 or less.

- **Use A Checklist** - Put all the copy you write through a copywriting checklist, which can be an excellent way to make sure you maintain a standard of high quality. Either create your own custom checklist, or find one online by searching *Google* for *copywriting checklist.*

Manage Client Reviews

General Client Review

- **Don't Be An Arrogant Jerk** - Always be understanding of your clients' comments and feedback, even if you feel they don't understand the art of copywriting. Kindness is always better than arrogance.

- **Ask, Why?** - Ask for *specific* reasons why your client wants something changed. This will either help them to clarify to you what it is they do want, or it will help eliminate a 'knee-jerk' reaction they may have to something they don't fully appreciate or understand.

- **Choose Your Battles** - If you feel strongly about a change or critique, then speak up! You *are* the expert.

- **Always Copyright Your Material** - For any ads, emails, brochures, etc., that you send to your client, make sure you identify them with a copyright notice (© Copyright 2010 Your Corporation). This will deter unscrupulous clients from simply stealing your ideas without paying you for them.

Legal Review

- **Run It by The Lawyers** - Have the client (and/or their attorney) double-check any statements or claims containing the following words:

- Free

- Guaranteed

- Best, lowest, fastest, etc.

- Or your money back

- Risk-free

- No risk

- No purchase necessary

- No cost

- No obligation

- No investment

- 100 percent

- Promise

- No questions asked

Test

Test the following to achieve the best results:

- **Headlines** - Individual words, shorter vs. longer, questions vs. statements, font sizes and colors

- **Subheadlines** - Individual words, shorter vs. longer, questions vs. statements, font sizes and colors

- **Main Copy** - Longer vs. shorter, more bulleted lists vs. less

- **Lead** - Try different leads, long vs. short

- **Price** - Higher vs. lower, ending in .00 vs. .97 or .77

- **Guarantee** - Individual words, length of guarantee (90 days vs. 60 days vs. lifetime), guarantee graphic

- **Testimonials** - More vs. less, longer vs. shorter, photos vs. no photos

- **Call To Action** - Displaying credit card logos vs. not, the look of the order button, the text on the order button

- **Your P.S.** - Including one vs. not, the content of the P.S., a single P.S. vs. multiple P.S.'s

- **Bonuses** - More bonuses vs. fewer bonuses, the order of bonuses

- **Flow** - Move various elements up or down the page (make sure they still make sense in their new context)

- **Graphics** - More vs. fewer, switch graphics out, larger vs. smaller

- **Main Typeface** - Serif vs. san serif, font size, with of columns

Related Searches:

split testing copywriting

split testing tips - <u>Videos</u>

conversion tips - <u>Videos</u>

The
Copywriting
Business

Discover New Opportunities

- **Become An Expert** - When you focus your efforts on mastering how to write copy for a specific market or media, your value increases - specialists can usually charge more than generalists.

- **Do What You Love** - With so many varied opportunities in copywriting, there's a market for you to tap into that will excite you. Be adventurous and try different types of projects to get a feel for what suits you best.

Media Types

- **Landing (Squeeze) Page Copywriting** - Create highly-specialized Web pages that motivate a visitor to take immediate action of some sort, usually to enter their email address.

  Related Searches:

  landing page copy | copywriting

  landing page optimization tips

  landing page best practices

  landing page example

  landing page template

- **White Papers** - Create special reports that address specific challenges, as well as inform readers how to solve them, and make informed decisions. White papers tend to be more informational than promotional.

writing white papers

how to write white paper

white paper writing tips

white paper template

- **Press Releases** - Write announcements that are submitted to various news organizations in order to inform and publicize upcoming events, product releases, and promotions.

Related Searches:

how to write a press release

press release tips

sample press release

press release template

- **Email** - Write individual email announcements or a series of emails in a way that gets people to open and read them, and take action.

Related Searches:

email copywriting

email marketing tips - <u>Videos</u>

email marketing best practices

autoresponder tips

- **Twitter** - Help companies use Twitter, or other social marketing tools, to connect and communicate with their communities.

Related Searches:

twitter marketing guide

twitter marketing tips

twitter tips and tricks

- **Video** - Write compelling and emotionally engaging scripts for videos.

  Related Searches:

  video marketing tips - Videos

  how to create a viral video - Videos

  viral videos - Videos

- **PPC/AdWords** - Create short ads for companies to promote their products and services.

  Related Searches:

  adwords copywriting

  adwords tips

  adwords strategies

  ppc copywriting

  ppc tips

  ppc strategies

Markets

- **Technical** - Write copy that is geared more towards engineers, managers, and other technical people who require very specific, and often complex information.

technical writing

technical writing tips

technical writing jobs

- **SEO/Web** - Write copy for Websites, product pages, emails, or other online resources.

  Related Searches:

  seo copywriting

  seo copywriting tips

  seo copywriting jobs

- **Health** - Specialize in copy that appeals to people that are very interested in health-related topics - supplements, weight loss, alternative health, and so on.

  Related Searches:

  writing for the health | medical market

  health | medical writing jobs

- **B2B** - Write to the needs of business people, and their challenges to build and maintain profitable businesses.

  Related Searches:

  b2b writing

  b2b marketing

  b2b marketing tips

- **Travel** - Write about places, experiences, people, and cultures in a way that captures and holds the readers imagination.

Related Searches:

travel writing

travel writing jobs

writing for the travel industry

Market Your Business: Your Message

- **Remember That YOU Are The Product** - While your experience and client list are important, your most important marketing asset is your most unique asset - you! You need to determine your personal strengths and find a way to create a marketing messages that bridges the gap between those strengths and the value you can provide to a client.

Related Searches:

how to market yourself - Videos

ways to market yourself

creative ways to market yourself

- **Answer WIIFT** - Employers, just like other prospects, want to know less about you and your accomplishments, and more about WIIFT or, what's in it for them.

- **Be Consistent** - Decide on a message, identity, and personality for your business - use them consistently in all your marketing materials. This will help position you as the person known for X, and is an important part of establishing your brand.

Related Searches:

personal branding - Videos

personal branding tips - Videos

- **Keep It Positive** - Make sure your marketing materials convey confidence and positivity.

- **Show Your Personality** - If you portray yourself one way in your marketing, and another way in real-life, potential clients will pick up on it and begin wondering why. If you work from your rural home, enjoy the country, and have a lighthearted personality, don't try to come across like a city-dwelling, corporate shark in your marketing material. Simply be who you are!

Related Searches:

market | promote your business - <u>Videos</u>

Market Your Business: Your Business Cards

- **Go Double-Sided** - Choose a double-sided design. Use the front of your card for your company name, your name, and contact info (phone, email, URL), as well as a tagline (if you have one). On the back of the card include a headline with a link to a special report or white paper, or list your services, benefits, and some testimonials.

- **Keep Them Simple** - Don't fill your card with a lot of clutter. Identify the core message of your business and convey that. A link to your Website can be used to fill in the details.

- **Make Them Unique** - The best business cards are the one's that people want to show others, because they're so unique. Without going overboard, try to come up with a creative way to make your card stand out, either by its shape, the material on which it's printed, or the message it contains.

Related Searches:

unique | creative business cards - Images

google business cards - Images

- **Include Them In Your Mailings** - Add a couple of your business cards with mailings you send out, especially invoices. This can be a great way to encourage satisfied customers to spread the word about your products or services.

- **Always Carry Them With You** - Because you never know who you might run into while you're out and about, stuff a card holder with a stack of your cards and place it next to your car keys. That way you'll always remember to take your cards with you whenever you leave your house.

Related Searches:

business card holder - Shopping

- **Give And Get** - Whenever you give your business card to someone, it's considered proper etiquette to ask for theirs in return.

- **Be Generous** - No one says you can only give a single card away per person. Give 2 or 3 away to each person who is willing to take them.

Related Searches:

business cards [zip code or city name] - Local

business card tips - Videos

business card templates - Images

Market Your Business: Your Business Name

- **Brand You** - Choosing a great business name can be as simple as using your own name. You are unique, your name clearly identifies you, and by using your personal name it shows that you're willing to stake your personal reputation on the quality and service your business provides.

- **Have A Tagline** - In all your marketing materials, include a tagline with your company name - Identify your USP, and use it.

  Related Searches:

  how to write | create a tagline

  tagline examples

- **Avoid Cute, Clever Names** - If your business name makes people laugh, that's how people will see your business.

Related Searches:

how to choose a business | company name - Videos

business name generator

business name ideas

Market Your Business: Your Portfolio

- **Put It Online** - Focus on building an online presence for all your portfolio pieces. An online portfolio can be accessed by interested parties at their convenience, and you save money by not having to send samples via snail-mail. Check to make sure all your portfolio links are working.

- **Showcase Your Skills, Not Your Client List** - If you don't have 'real' client examples, then create some. You're goal is to showcase your writing skills, not the number of clients you've had. Just remember not to imply that a sample was for a company unless it really was.

- **Show Your Versatility** - Provide a variety of examples in your portfolio to showcase the versatility of your skills.

- **Front-Load It** - Design your portfolio so your best work appears first, followed by your second-best, and so on.

- **Use The End-Result** - Ask your clients for copies of the final materials that are sent to their prospects/customers (print or digital).

- **Add It If You Wrote It** - Everything you write should be considered a portfolio piece - sales letters, blog posts, articles, personal promotions, etc.

- **Remove The So-So Examples** - Don't include a project just because you have it, and you can. If it's not your best work, then leave it out.

- **Highlight VIP Projects** - Highlight any work you've done for notables, such as heavyweights in an industry, celebrities, notable companies, etc.

- **Schedule A Time For Updates** - Pick a date once a month, or every quarter, when you will update and maintain your portfolio. Be consistent with this process so that your portfolio always reflects the quality and high standards of your business.

- **Draw Inspiration From Other Copywriters** - Go to *Google* and do a search for *copywriting | copywriter portfolio*. Click on some of the results to see how other copywriters display their portfolio. Use the best ideas you discover for creating your own portfolio.

Related Searches:

how to portfolio page | site – <u>Videos</u>

portfolio tips

portfolio design

portfolio design templates

Improve Your Skills: Maintain A Swipe File

- **Appreciate The Importance Of A Good Swipe File** - A swipe file provides inspiration and ideas for those times when you're faced with writer's block. It can also help you complete projects faster, as you can draw from facts and research that's already been discovered.

  Related Searches:

  overcome writer's block - Videos

- **Collect Success** - Maintain a swipe file of million-dollar sales letters, magalogs, and other successful ads that you discover.

  Related Searches:

  collection | archive | best ads - Videos

- **Watch Infomercials** - Infomercials may be annoying to most people, including you, but as a copywriter, you should appreciate that you're actually watching great copy come to life with video. Study infomercials, and think about how they are emotionally appealing, demonstrate benefits, and how they flow from beginning to end.

  Related Searches:

  infomercials - Videos

  top | best infomercials - Videos

  as seen on tv - Videos

- **Look At Magazine Covers** - Magazine covers are some of the best resources for great headlines. They're designed to capture a person's attention, and draw them into wanting to pick up the magazine to read more, which is exactly what you want to learn how to do. Celebrity, teen, money, travel, and health-related magazines display some of the best ideas.

Related Searches:

magazines

magazines online

magazine covers - Images

[magazine name] magazine covers - Images

- **Subscribe To Swipe** - Subscribe to publications and newsletters that consistently create great copy.

- **Order Catalogs** - Request catalogs to be sent to you from businesses such as *JC Penny* and *SkyMall*. Catalogs are typically full of great copy ideas!

Related Searches:

catalogs

catalogs online

- **Study digg.com Headlines** - Visit *digg.com* and pay attention to the headlines for the most popular stories. Model your headlines on them - figure out what makes them work. Try substituting the topic within a good headline with yours, using word-substitution.

- **Build A Virtual Swipe File** - Use Web-based note-capturing tools (try *www.evernote.com*) for grabbing online copy that you find inspirational.

Related Searches:

evernote tutorial | tips - Videos

- **Keep Your Swipe File In Order** - You can organize your files by the type of product being sold (merchandise, subscription, etc.), product categories (travel, health, etc.), or the type of offer (cash, bill me later, etc.)

- **Maximize Your Use Of Your Swipe File** - Review your swipe file any time you need ideas for a headline or bullets, or for the structure and flow of your copy.

- **Pay Attention To Bullets** - Find common ideas and bullets found in multiple letters within a niche and make sure your copy includes those. They are hot-button elements for that niche.

- **Stick With Your Niche** - Swipe from letters and ads that sell to your target market. In other words, don't swipe a financial letter or ad for ideas on writing copy for a health product.

- **Don't Plagiarize** - Swipe ideas and concepts, NOT the actual copy!

Related Searches:

swipe files

free swipe files

Improve Your Skills: Practice

- **Be A Student Of Great Copy** - Study content, flow, styling (colors, fonts, bolding, underlining, etc.), use of bullets, Johnson boxes, graphics, etc., of great copy used in print, TV/video, and radio/audio).

- **Get Into The Minds Of Great Copywriters** - Hand-write great sales copy, word-for-word. This practice will help put you in the same mindset as the original writer and greatly improve your skills.

- **Dissect Great Copy** - As you read great copy, make notes with your observations in the margin. Ask plenty of 'why' questions; Why is this here? Why is this effective?

- **Dissect Bad Copy** - Go through bad copy and determine what's missing, or what you would add or change to make it stronger.

- **Practice, Practice, Practice** - Write a 50-100 word lead every day.

Improve Your Skills:
Other Ideas

- **Write With Passion** - If you're not excited about what you're writing, don't expect your reader to be. You *must* develop a passion for your current project, even if it's temporary.

- **Experiment A Little** - Following 'accepted' copywriting rules will only get you so far. Don't be afraid to experiment with new styles and ideas, even if it means taking some criticism.

- **Welcome Feedback** - Learn to thrive on criticism. You might learn something!

- **Master These 3 Elements** - Focus on mastering these 3 key elements of great copy:

> - Discovering ideas that excite your readers
>
> - Expressing your ideas clearly and simply
>
> - Proving your ideas beyond a reasonable doubt

Managing & Growing Your Business: Finding Clients

- **Fire Liars** - If a client ever asks you to lie in your copy, drop them instantly! If they have no problem being dishonest to their customers, they'll have no problem doing the same to you. Working with a client like this could also lead to you becoming involved with something that could easily damage your personal or business reputation.

Find Clients - The Step-By-Step System

1. **Do Some Research** - Research 10 companies you think you'd like to work for (target companies that would recognize the benefit of copywriting), then narrow your list down to your top 3.

2. **Get The Right Contact Info** - Find out the name and contact information for the person that hires freelancers.

3. **Analyze Their Needs** - Research your top 3 companies - their needs, market, current marketing materials, and their competitors.

4. **Discover Their Weakness** - Define an area of weakness and determine what solution you would be able to provide.

5. **Provide Them With The Solution** - Send a personal letter to the person in charge of hiring. Offer something of value to them - a white paper, report, or free consultation - related to your solution.

6. **Talk Less, Listen More** - When you're contacted, do more listening and less talking. Discover their needs and offer some of

your ideas for solutions.

7. **Let Them Know What You Can Do For Them** - Offer to send a proposal of your services and fees. Don't offer a price over the phone.

8. **Say Thank You** - Send a personal thank you. It's best if it's handwritten.

9. **Don't Be A Pest** - Once you've sent your proposal and thank you, then give your potential client plenty of time to respond on their own. If you follow-up every day, or every other day, you'll accomplish little more than annoying them.

Find Clients - Other Methods To Try

- **Post An Ad On craigslist.org** – *craigslist.org* is one of the largest sources of classified ads on the planet. Many writers post ads advertising their services. Why don't you?

  Related Searches:

  craigslist posting tips - Videos

  how to post on craigslist - Videos

- **Search craigslist.org For Jobs** - Since *craigslist.org* doesn't allow you to search all locations at the same time, go to *Google* and enter the search: *site:craigslist.org freelance copywriter | copywriting.* You discover a number of recent freelance copywriting jobs with this technique.

- **Do A Google Search** - Go to *Google* and search for *freelance copywriting jobs.* Explore the many results that appear and bookmark any resources that stand out. Many services you find will provide the ability for you to sign up for email alerts of new job listings, so look for those.

- **Provide Help In Forums** - Visit forums that cater to the types of clients you want to attract. Post useful information and answers. Don't directly promote your services, but use your forum signature to offer a free report or link to a tips page on your business site.

- **Look For Local Opportunities** - Regularly check your local paper for news about companies that are announcing new products, services, or partnerships. Every story is a potential opportunity for you to build your business.

Related Searches:

how to find copywriting clients | jobs

Managing & Growing Your Business: Your Fees

- **Charge By The Project, Not By The Hour** - Charging an hourly rate is too subjective and opens up your fee to 'negotiation' when the client feels your time estimate is wrong. Charge by the project, then figure out ways to streamline your copywriting process in order to maximize your profits.

- **Get A Raise** - Raise your fees when you have so much business that you can afford to lose clients unwilling to pay your new rates.

- **Don't Post Your Fees Online** - Fee amounts posted on a Web page are captured by search engines and can be shown in search results many years after you've raised them.

- **Be Flexible** - If you're just starting out, it's OK to be flexible with your rates in order to land some business. Just don't sell yourself too short.

- **Make A Value Estimation** - Consider the value of the project to your client when charging for a project. It makes sense to charge more money for projects that can potentially make your client a lot of money.

- **Start Small** - Consider initially charging a smaller rate for a client that has potential long-term value. After you've established your worth to them, begin charging more.

- **Always Get What You're Worth** - Never ask for less than what you're worth just to get a job. Never sell yourself short!

Related Searches:

copywriting fees

Managing & Growing Your Business: Negotiating

- **Ask Plenty Of Questions** - Get to know your potential client, what they want, what they do, and the outcome they expect. The greater your clarity, the better you'll be able to deliver the results they want.

- **Deliver Results, But Don't Promise Them** - Never promise a client a specific results. It's impossible to guarantee a specific response or result.

- **Get Half Now** - Get at least half your fees upfront, and the other half upon delivery of the copy manuscript. Most reputable clients will have no problem with this.

- **Get It In Writing** - Only perform work after you have a signed contract/proposal for the project. Don't rely on verbal commitments.

- **Be Specific** - Make it clear in the proposal what you agree to deliver - nothing more, nothing less.

- **Give Yourself Plenty Of Time** - Ask for at least a week more than you need for each project. Something almost always gets in the way of a deadline. If you can deliver it before then, your client will think you're amazing.

- **Always Explain The Value Associated With A Fee** - Remember your skills as a copywriter when delivering your invoice. Make sure you've clearly defined the value the client has received for the fees you charge.

Managing & Growing Your Business: Keeping Clients Happy

- **Keep Correspondences Short** - Your clients are like everyone else, they don't like wasting their time on emails that are full of a lot of unnecessary fluff. When communicating with your clients, don't spend a lot of time on small talk - get to the point quickly.

Related Searches:

how to write emails

email etiquette

- **Under-Promise And Over-Deliver** - Anything you can do to make your client feel as though you went *way* over what was expected will not only impress in their minds your true value to them, but likely create a sense in them to reciprocate by giving you more work.

- **Keep Your Complaining To Yourself** - Most clients have no interest whatsoever in being a shoulder for you to cry on. If you've had a lousy day, you're sick, or your refrigerator just quit, be sure to keep it to yourself. Instead, be as positive and upbeat with them as you possibly can.

- **Don't Brag** - You may be one of the top 3 greatest copywriters in the Midwest, and you may be personal friends with the other 2, but constantly bragging about what you know, and who you know, means very little to your client after they've hired you - you've convinced them already. After they hire you, all that matters are the results you achieve.

- **Be Respectful** - Clients say and do some crazy things from time-to-time. Unless you sense that they're trying to be funny, don't laugh at their ideas, or belittle their efforts - they don't like it!

- **Be Consistent** - If you provide a client with great service, then miserable service, chances are, they'll remember the miserable. To keep your clients happy, you need to consistently provide great service - they need to know they can rely on you every time.

- **Be Timely** - If your client has a problem, and they email you or leave you a voicemail, then get back to them as soon as you possibly can. There are few things that are more frustrating to them than to have to wait on a response from you when they're in a stressful state.

- **Remember To Say Thank You** - After completing a project for a client, always be sure to send them a personal thank you. This does a lot to help create a trusting, favorable relationship.

- **Ask For Feedback** - If you want to improve your client's experience when working with you, there's no better way of learning how to then to ask them for feedback and suggestions. Ask them directly for feedback, or send out a survey.

Related Searches:

online surveys

- **Send Them An Email** - Occasionally sending a short, simple email to a client to see how they're doing is a great way of reminding them you that you care, and that you exist, which may be just the trigger needed for them to consider hiring you for a project they have in front of them.

- **Give Them Something Valuable** - Send clients a free ebook with valuable information (top 10 tips, trends, mistakes to avoid) or provide a link to a site that contains something they might find useful. Whatever you do, don't make what you send them a promotional tool in disguise. Use *Google Alerts* to be notified whenever something relevant is posted online.

Related Searches:

google alerts - Videos

- **Recognize Them Publicly** - Thanking your clients publicly, such as on your Website, blog, or newsletter, allows you to express your appreciation for their business in a way that reflects positively on them someplace where everyone can see it.

- **Shoot For Quality Over Quantity** - It's better to service a small number of clients *really* well than it is to service a lot of clients so-so.

- **Always Deliver Quality** - Everything your client receives from you should be of the highest quality - documents should be well-formatted, spell checked, and links should work.

Copywriting Resources

Copywriting Searches

Discover tons of great copywriting related content (blogs, articles, videos, etc.) online by typing the search terms (on the left) into the tools indicated (on the right).

Top Copywriters

ted nicholas - Google, YouTube

gary halbert - Google, YouTube

bob bly - Google, YouTube

dan kennedy - Google, YouTube

john carlton - Google, YouTube

michel fortin - Google, YouTube

gary bencivenga - Google

clayton makepeace - Google

ken mccarthy - Google

General Copywriting

copywriting - Google, YouTube, Yahoo Answers (answers.yahoo.com), Scribd (www.scribd.com)

copywriting tips - Google, YouTube, Scribd

copywriting how to - Google, YouTube, Yahoo Answers

copywriting newsletter - Google

copywriting secrets - Google, YouTube

copywriting articles - Google

copywriting checklist - Google

copywriting blog - Google

copywriting forum - Google

copywriting jobs - Google

headline formulas - Google

About The Author

Derek Franklin is a writer, copywriter, consultant, software developer, and all-around creative thinker.

His mission in life is to help people understand and use ideas and strategies that can have a positive effect on their lives and the results they achieve in their lives.

Derek began his journey helping others in 1998, when he created a series of online tutorials that showed others how to use Adobe Flash. This lead to his first book deal - a how-to book on Flash for Macromedia Press (now Adobe Press).

Since that time, Derek has achieved a number of milestones:

- Written 5 best-selling books on the topic of Adobe Flash that have sold over 250,000 copies in more than a dozen languages worldwide

- Worked as Creative Director for a nationally recognized company, with clients that included Adidas and Papa Johns

- Created several software products used by 1000's of satisfied users

- Launched more than 15 projects online - everything from software, to ebooks, to a membership site

For more information about Derek, as well as his other products and services, visit www.derekfranklin.com.